FAMILIES IN
DANGER

FAMILIES IN DANGER

PROTECTING YOUR FAMILY IN AN X-RATED WORLD

RANDAL A. WRIGHT

Deseret Book Company
Salt Lake City, Utah

©1988 Randal A. Wright
All rights reserved
Printed in the United States of America

No part of this book may be reproduced in any
form or by any means without permission in writing
from the publisher, Deseret Book Company,
P.O. Box 30178, Salt Lake City, Utah 84130.

First printing March 1988

Library of Congress Cataloging-in-Publication Data

Wright, Randal A.
    Families in danger : protecting your family in an X-rated world /
by Randal A. Wright.
      p.   cm.
    Includes bibliographies and index.
    ISBN 0-87579-129-8 : $9.95 (est.)
    1. Child rearing—Religious aspects—Mormon Church. 2. Mass media
and children—United States—Moral and ethical aspects.   I. Title.
HQ769.3.W74   1988   87-36591
649'.1—dc19   CIP

CONTENTS

	Preface	vii
1	Follow the Brethren	1
2	Latter-day Deceit	13
3	Heroes and Peer Pressure	23
4	The Most Successful School System	39
5	Learning to Control TV	51
6	Rating the Movies	73
7	The Challenge of Modern Music	91
8	Protecting Our Communities	105
9	Helping Youth Stay Morally Clean	115
10	"Inspire Them to Greatness"	127
	Index	139

PREFACE

We live in an exciting but very challenging world. Never before in history have so many inventions been available for the benefit and enjoyment of mankind. Through these modern miracles, we have been blessed with more leisure time than ever before. Yet, in an attempt to use this added time, many have only increased their pace of living, rather than effectively using the added moments of leisure to strengthen themselves and their families. Never before have families had so many options to choose from in planning how to use their time and money. As a result, the most basic and fundamental unit of society, the family itself, has been placed in extreme danger. What is causing such pressures on families? What can we do to protect ourselves and stay strong?

President Ezra Taft Benson pointed out the dangers we face when he said:

> We live in a wicked world. Never in our memory have the forces of evil been arrayed in such deadly formation. The devil is well organized. Never in our day has he had so many emissaries working for him. Through his many agents, his satanic majesty has proclaimed his intentions to destroy one whole generation of our choice young people. Evidence of the dastardly work of evil forces is increasingly evident. On every side we see the sad and heart-rending results. The devil-inspired destructive forces are present in our literature, in our art, in the movies, on the radio, in our dress, in our dances, on the TV screen, and even in our modern, so-called popular music. Satan uses many tools to weaken and destroy the home and family and especially our young people. Today,

as never before, it seems the devil's thrust is directed at our youth.[1]

Several years ago my wife and I rented a house that had been placed on the market to be sold. I had personally painted this home for the owners and inspected it closely to be sure it was in good shape. Everything looked in order to me, so the owners proceeded to list the home with a realtor. Soon a buyer was located and the loan papers began to be processed. As part of the loan procedure, inspectors were sent to check the condition of the home. I was surprised when these experts found not only evidence of termites, but a cracked foundation as well. I could hardly believe their report, since the home appeared in perfect shape to me. I soon found that the problem with my inspection was that I hadn't known what to look for. When I learned how to inspect for damage, I was able to see the evidence that confirmed the experts' diagnosis. After some effort and expense, the owners were able to correct the problems and the home was quickly sold.

Since this experience, I have frequently thought of the need for some type of checklist for the spiritual foundations of our homes. We may do well to ask ourselves when was the last time we closely checked that foundation. Was there evidence of cracking? Do we know how to identify the spiritual termites that seem to be destroying so many families in our society? This book is an effort to help us check our family foundations, identify some of the sources of our problems, and offer possible suggestions in dealing with them. Obviously, we cannot deal with all the challenges and problems that face us. In fact, we can consider only a few of the potential problem areas. But in my research and work with the youth, the evidence keeps pointing to these specific areas as a source of many of the difficulties families face, difficulties that seem to be taking a tremendous spiritual, as well as physical, toll on many families, and especially on youth. I have tried to present this information in an interesting and uplifting manner. But remember, we must look closely at the evidence, and sometimes this is not pleasant to consider. The seriousness of the problem has prompted this examination.

The words of King Benjamin to the people of his day seem to apply here. I truly believe they were written for our day as well. He said: "And finally, I cannot tell you all the things whereby ye may commit sin; for there are divers ways and means, even so many that I cannot number them. But this much I can tell you, that if ye do not watch yourselves, and your thoughts, and your words, and your deeds, and observe the commandments of God, and continue in the faith of what ye have heard concerning the coming of our Lord, even unto the end of your lives, ye must perish. And now, O man, remember, and perish not." (Mosiah 4:29-30.)

May we each watch our thoughts, our words, and our actions, and strive to keep the commandments of God, so that our home's foundations will remain strong.

NOTE

1. Ezra Taft Benson, *God, Family, Country: Our Three Great Loyalties* (Salt Lake City: Deseret Book, 1974), p. 243.

CHAPTER 1

FOLLOW THE BRETHREN

Several years ago my brother Jack bought a go-cart for his sons for Christmas. He lives in a neighborhood that has approximately thirty children under the age of sixteen, so you can imagine the excitement the go-cart produced. Every time one of the boys would get on to take a ride, about fifteen other kids would be running behind begging for a turn.

After Jack, my father, and I had observed the scene for a short time, we found a solution to the problem of who should take the next turn. In a nearby open field, we marked off a circular go-cart track. We then told the kids to get in a line and wait their turn for a ride around the oval track. My brother helped each new rider settle into the go-cart and then pushed it to get a fast start, while my father and I enjoyed watching.

Everything was going fine until Jack's son Shay, age six, got on for his turn. He was very excited, grinning from ear to ear. When he was situated on the cart, Jack asked him if he was ready to go. He answered by pushing the gas pedal all the way down and taking off. The neighborhood kids roared their approval as the tires spun on his quick start.

The track we had marked off was circular, but as Shay neared the first curve, he didn't turn when he was expected to and proceeded on a straight course instead. The children cheered even louder, thinking this was really exciting. But three adults were viewing the same scene in terror, for Shay was headed straight toward a busy major highway. Seeing the danger his son was in, Jack took off as fast as he could, sprinting after the speeding vehicle. The crowd still cheered in the background, not realizing the peril facing their friend.

Just before Shay reached the highway, he turned the wheels and headed back toward the track. This allowed Jack to cut his lead and come within a few feet of the go-cart. But the chase was still on, as the father tried desperately to catch his speeding son. Then, as suddenly as it had begun, the chase was over. As Shay glanced triumphantly at his friends, the cart ran head-on into a tree. On impact, Shay's head went forward, slamming his mouth and nose into the steering wheel. Jack was running so fast behind him that he couldn't stop and crashed into the back of the go-cart, banging both legs at shin level.

By this time the crowd had settled down and there was no longer excitement in the air as the battered go-cart rested against the tree and a bloody six-year-old walked toward us with his badly limping father.

I've reflected a lot about that experience and have since concluded that it is not unlike the situation in some of our families. How many of us as parents do essentially the same thing with our own children that my brother did with his? Like the go-cart ride, we spend little or no time instructing and training our children on how to navigate safely through the perilous journey called youth. Many teenagers embark upon their dating years about the way Shay did on his go-cart ride, grinning from ear to ear, but unprepared for the temptations and dangers facing them. When dangers do come, many of their peers, like Shay's neighbors, cheer them on through peer pressure. When parents finally realize the tremendous risks their children are facing, they often go chasing after them. Unfortunately, many times both the youth and the parents become seriously hurt, as was Shay. Occasionally one of the young people even ventures out onto a spiritual highway and is hit. Others are seriously injured, and some are even lost. In many cases they could have been saved, if parents had only trained and prepared them better, while they were young, for the "ride" they would one day take.

Heavenly Father expects us to teach and protect these spirits who have been placed in our care. One man put it this way:

> I was standing in Tiffany's great store in New York, and I heard the salesman say to a lady who had asked him about some pearls, "Madam, this pearl is worth $17,000." I was interested at once. I said, "Let me see the pearl that is worth $17,000." The salesman put it on a piece of black cloth, and I studied it carefully. I said, "I suppose Tiffany's stock is very valuable." And as I looked around that beautiful store, I imagined them bringing all their stock up to my house and saying, "We want you to take care of this tonight." What do you think I would do? I would go as quickly as I could to the telephone and call up the chief of police, and say, "I have all Tiffany's stock in my house, and it is too great a responsibility. Will you send some of your most trusted officers to help me?" You would do the same, wouldn't you? But I have a little boy in my home, and for him I am responsible. I have had him for nine years, and some of you may have just such another little boy. I turn to this old Book and I read this word: "What is a man profited if he shall gain the whole world, and lose his own soul? or what shall a man give in exchange for his soul?" [Matthew 16:26.] It is as if he had all the diamonds and rubies and pearls in the world, and held them in one hand, and just put a little boy in the other, and the boy would be worth more than all the jewels. If you would tremble because you had seventeen thousand dollars' worth of jewels in your house one night, how shall you go up to your Father and the lad be not with you?[1]

While I was growing up, we used to laugh at how loud my father snored. I remember once asking my mother if his snoring ever bothered her. I was surprised at her comment: she actually said she never knew he snored. I thought she was kidding, but I soon learned that she was not. I wondered how that could be possible. How, with the bed almost shaking, could she lie beside him and read a book and never hear a thing? Occasionally, when I would walk into their room with my father snoring and my mother reading, I would ask her if she could hear him then. She would laugh and admit she could hear him if I pointed it out to her. I thought how strange it was that she could go for all those years and never notice the noise until it was pointed out.

A few years ago I began to understand better what my mother had meant when she said she wasn't bothered by his snoring. My wife and I bought a home on a piece of commercial property with hopes of selling it one day for a profit and buying the home we really wanted. The house was in a very high traffic district, and visitors often asked how we could bear living in this area with the constant roar outside. We would usually answer that we must be used to it because we never noticed the noise. I could tell by the looks we received that many considered this very strange.

One night my wife and I were discussing some of the dangers that modern families face. Since I work with youth and deal with their challenges daily, I pointed out how some of us as parents seem to be asleep to these dangers, even though we are active in the Church and should realize the threats. As we talked, I thought of the fact that my mother couldn't recognize that my father was snoring until it was pointed out, and that we too had failed to recognize the noise from the traffic passing by our home. Was it possible that destructive forces were influencing our families and we were not even able to recognize the danger? It was a frightening thought. Together we read a statement from President Spencer W. Kimball that further alarmed us to the dangers we face. He said:

> [There] are Church members who are steeped in lethargy. They neither drink nor commit the sexual sins. They do not gamble nor rob nor kill. They are good citizens and splendid neighbors, but spiritually speaking they seem to

be in a long, deep sleep. They are doing nothing seriously wrong except in their failures to do the right things to earn their exaltation. To such people as this, the words of Lehi might well apply: "O that ye would awake; awake from a deep sleep, yea, even from the sleep of hell, and shake off the awful chains by which ye are bound." (2 Nephi 1:13.)[2]

We spent considerable time that night discussing areas in which we had been negligent with our own family, and the challenges that other families may face. After words I spent a miserable and sleepless night. I had never noticed so much noise and commotion: cars and trucks roaring by, horns honking, tires squealing, dogs barking, the wind blowing through the trees, and the dripping faucet all became so noticeable that sleep was impossible. I clearly saw that we all need to be aware of the temptations placed before us and our families—and especially our teens and young adults—if we are to avoid these trials.

By daylight I vowed that I didn't want to be in the third category described by Nicholas Butler, who said there are only three kinds of people: (1) those who make things happen; (2) those who watch things happen; and (3) those who have no idea what is happening.

I pledged to myself that night that I would try to identify and study some of the dangers placed in our path and try to find solutions, if possible. I am convinced that if we were to identify all the techniques being used in our day, Satan would find new ones to replace them. But three areas in particular stand out: movies, television, and music—and more specifically, the inappropriate variety. If we are to be protected from their influence, we must be alert and heed the words of our living prophets.

If I have learned any lesson in my own life and in my study of the scriptures, it is this: Blessings and safety come to us if we follow the prophets, and consequences result when we go against their inspired teachings. President Harold B. Lee expressed it this way:

> Now the only safety we have as members of this church

is to do exactly what the Lord said to the Church in that day when the Church was organized. We must learn to give heed to the words and commandments that the Lord shall give through his prophet, "as he receiveth them, walking in all holiness before me; . . . as if from mine own mouth, in all patience and faith." (D&C 21:4-5.) There will be some things that take patience and faith. You may not like what comes from the authority of the Church. It may contradict your political views. It may contradict your social views. It may interfere with some of your social life. . . . Your safety and ours depends upon whether or not we follow the ones whom the Lord has placed to preside over his church. He knows whom he wants to preside over this church, and he will make no mistake. The Lord doesn't do things by accident. . . . Let's keep our eye on the President of the Church.[3]

I know, from my own experience, this statement is true. Many of us can take instruction well unless it contradicts our social or political views or interferes with our social life. For example, some teenagers have no problems accepting counsel and instruction from their basketball or football coach, but they have a hard time accepting the church authorities' teachings on not single dating during their early dating years. A person may do quite well accepting counsel related to ballet, art, drama, or speech, but struggle with and even reject the church authorities' teachings on not listening to inappropriate music. It seems that instruction and counsel are welcomed and even sought after in areas like basketball, yet we sometimes ignore or even refuse to listen to advice in the crucial areas of our lives.

One day I decided to try to teach this lesson to the ones who had made me aware of it to begin with — my early-morning seminary class. To do this, I asked my wife to dress up our little three-year-old daughter, Natalie, in her nicest outfit. Then I put my sleepy little girl in the car and off we went to my 5:55 A.M. class. Before class Natalie sat in the laps of several students, as I had hoped she would. About halfway through class, I brought her to the front of the room and sat her on the table in front of everyone. I reminded the class that my wife was about to have another baby and asked if any of them would be willing to take care of Natalie after school for the few days that my wife would be in the hospital. Most of the students volunteered to do so.

After some discussion, I singled out one young woman that I thought needed a lesson on following the counsel of her church leaders. I said, "Angie, would you take care of Natalie for us?" She replied, "Yes, I'd be glad to." I then explained to her that I was a very protective father and would want her to watch my daughter very closely, because when she was smaller, she had occasionally gone toward the busy street. Angie promised to keep a close watch on her. I then asked what she would do if Natalie started walking toward the street. She said, "I'd tell her to come back." I replied, "What if Natalie told you to leave her alone, that she would go if she wanted to?" Angie replied that she would go get her and bring her back anyway. Then I asked what she would do if Natalie cried and screamed and told her to leave her alone—that she could play in the street if she wanted to. Angie said, "Look, I'll do whatever it takes to keep your little girl out of the street, even if I have to drag her back. You don't need to worry about her if I keep her."

I had received the very answer I had been seeking. I then explained that Heavenly Father knew when he sent us to earth that there would be many dangers and temptations placed in our paths—or busy streets, so to speak. For this reason he placed guides on earth to help us stay away from the danger. These guides are called parents, teachers, and prophets, and in a sense, they are our babysitters placed here to help us avoid danger.

I asked, "When these leaders see us going toward the busy streets of temptation or actually playing in the middle of the highway of sin, what should they do?" All of the students agreed they should warn us. I told them that that is exactly what these leaders are trying to do. They warn us not to play in the highway of sin, or we may be seriously injured spiritually. We may even be killed. But unlike Angie, these leaders can only warn us of the dangers; they cannot force us away from sin, because that would be tampering with our free agency. Then I concluded that none of us should be offended when we are given counsel that may be critical to our very salvation. We must keep our eye on the prophet if we are to avoid the hazards of the busy highways of sin that Satan has placed in our paths in these last days. That morning in seminary, I believe that we all realized the importance of taking counsel from those assigned to watch over us and keep us safe.

How are *we* — you and I — at taking instruction? Do we have an easier time following the counsel of a coach than we do our living prophet? We must never forget how critical it is to follow his counsel, if we are going to make it through the test of life safely. President Spencer W. Kimball gave us safety instructions when he said: "Every normal person may have a sure way of knowing what is right and what is wrong. He may learn the gospel and receive the Holy Spirit which will always guide him as to right and wrong. In addition to this, he has the leaders of the Lord's Church. And the only sure, safe way is to follow that leadership — follow the Holy Spirit within you and follow the prophets, dead and living."[4]

Imagine the following scene. You are casually driving home one evening after work, and as you look out the window to your left, you notice a frightening black cloud in the sky. You turn on the radio quickly to catch a weather report. A radio announcer is urgently warning of a gigantic tornado headed directly toward your city. Over and over you hear the warning and instructions on what to do to protect yourself. In buildings with no basements, the announcer says, a person should lie flat beneath a table or bed, away from windows. Arriving home, you find your family at the door waiting for you. They are all crying. They tell you the news you have just heard and repeat the instructions that have been given: a person should lie flat beneath a table or bed, away from the windows.

At this point what would you, as a parent, instruct your family to do?

1. Go to your local video rental shop to try to find a good movie to watch?

2. Sit down and read the newspaper?
3. Check the schedule to see what's playing on TV?
4. Play games on the computer?
5. Read the latest best-selling novel?
6. Take a nap?
7. Call a friend to learn the latest gossip?
8. Play some music on your stereo?
9. Go shopping?
10. Lie flat under a table or bed, away from the windows?

Most people would, of course, choose the last of these options. It would seem absurd to make any other choice. Yet, isn't a gigantic tornado exactly what is coming toward us in the last days? Satan may change the names, but the danger is the same. The tornado is called sin and apathy, and it is leaving destruction and misery in its path. This storm is very real. The number of casualties is staggering, yet many are choosing not to follow the instructions for safety provided by our prophets.

In 1940 public school officials were asked to name what they saw as the top discipline problems in their schools. In 1982 these officials were asked the same questions. Here are the results[5]:

1940
1. Talking
2. Chewing gum
3. Making noise
4. Running in the halls
5. Getting out of turn in line
6. Wearing improper clothing
7. Not putting paper in wastebasket

1982
1. Rape
2. Robbery
3. Assault
4. Burglary
5. Arson
6. Bombings
7. Murder
8. Suicide
9. Absenteeism
10. Vandalism
11. Extortion
12. Drugs
13. Alcohol
14. Gang warfare
15. Pregnancy
16. Abortion
17. Venereal disease

It would probably be safe to say that the problems our schools face are a reflection of our homes and society. The obvious question, then, is: Why the tremendous change in discipline problems from 1940 to 1982? Do you believe the discipline problems that occurred in the schools of 1776 at the beginning of this nation's history were much different from those reported in 1940? Probably not. Then how do we explain the enormous differences between the problems reported in 1940 and those reported in 1982? I'm sure there are various reasons for this drastic change, and it would be difficult to identify and explain all the reasons. But one thing is obvious. The tornado of sin and destruction is real in our day. Immorality in the United States is rampant. One source of these dramatic changes is the deterioration of standards in the media—movies, television, music, magazines. The media are very powerful tools that can influence people for good or evil. Kieth Merrill, a well-known Latter-day Saint movie director, has said, "We're not even remotely aware of how influenced we are by the media. [They are] *so pervasive*."[6]

Yes, the media are very powerful, but the tools themselves are not the problem. It is how they are being used. We should keep in mind that the hand of the Lord has been involved in major developments in the media. Priesthood holders have been directly involved in the development of sound on film, the television picture tube, and the satellite. We now have the potential to reach more people in one night through broadcasting via satellite than our missionaries have reached in more than 150 years through knocking on doors. The great tools of the media will be used to preach the gospel to every creature. Church authorities realize this power and have a communications system in place to spread the gospel to the world.

But let's not forget that someone else realizes the tremendous power of the media. Actor Gordon Jump made this observation: "There is no question in my mind that the Lord has his direct hand in the inventions of today. But the adversary has an incredible understanding of how to use the media."[7]

A tremendous battle rages between the forces of good and

evil, as we approach the Second Coming, and the media play major roles in this battle. Sheri L. Dew has written, "The battle for the minds of men that began with the war in heaven, continues today. But time is short, and many remain to be influenced. The media is perhaps the last great battlefront."[8]

President Ezra Taft Benson also identified the media as a source of temptation in an address to Aaronic Priesthood holders in April 1986:

> Consider carefully the words of the prophet Alma to his errant son, Corianton, "Forsake your sins, and go no more after the lusts of your eyes." (Alma 39:9.) "The lusts of your eyes." In our day, what does that expression mean? Movies, television programs, and video recordings that are both suggestive and lewd. Magazines and books that are obscene and pornographic. We counsel you, young men, not to pollute your minds with such degrading matter, for the mind through which this filth passes is never the same afterwards. Don't see R-rated movies or vulgar videos or participate in any entertainment that is immoral, suggestive, or pornographic.[9]

The amount of time Americans spend with the media is staggering. Movies, television, and music have great appeal, yet these tools, when used for the wrong reasons, can be a source of many temptations, as President Benson has warned. Many of the problems facing our schools and society are the very things glamorized in the media. How can we, as parents, help neutralize these temptations? Again, there is one comforting safety net provided for those who will give heed. It is called following the prophet. President Wilford Woodruff taught: "When counsel comes we should not treat it lightly, no matter to what subject it pertains, for if we do it will work evil unto us."[10]

Let us resolve that we and the members of our families will avoid anything that our prophets have warned us against. In a very literal sense, what they instruct us to do is what the Lord is actually saying to us, for he has declared, "Whether by mine own voice or by the voice of my servants, it is the same." (D&C 1:38.)

If our families are to avoid the trials and temptations of the last days, we must follow the brethren.

NOTES

1. J. Wilbur Chapman, *Better Homes and Families* (Wrights Enterprises, 1982), p. 8.
2. Spencer W. Kimball, *The Miracle of Forgiveness* (Salt Lake City: Bookcraft, 1969), pp. 211-12.
3. *Conference Report,* October 1970, pp. 152-53.
4. Spencer W. Kimball, May 14, 1968, "In the World But Not of It," *BYU Speeches of the Year,* 1968, pp. 11-12.
5. *Harper's Magazine*, March 1985, p. 25.
6. Sheri L. Dew, "To Every People," *This People*, February/March 1983, p. 27.
7. Ibid.
8. Ibid., p. 30.
9. *Ensign*, May 1986, p. 45.
10. *Journal of Discourses* 14:33.

CHAPTER 2

LATTER-DAY DECEIT

During my junior high school days, I had a good friend named Jimmy. He was a very creative person, but unfortunately, he sometimes used his talent in less than ideal ways to annoy and pester others, especially his teachers, with playful pranks. I learned over the years to stay clear of most of his ideas and schemes because they usually ended up causing trouble. One day, however, he came up with what I considered a fool-proof plan. I just couldn't resist becoming involved in it, although I knew we would be taking the risk of getting into trouble with our school officials.

Between the fourth wing of our school and the football stadium was a large practice field. You could see this field plainly from the classrooms in the fourth wing. One day Jimmy told about thirty of us boys to meet him out on the field during our lunch break. There he told us his plan and gave us specific instructions to help carry it out.

Our assignment was to form a circle around Jimmy and Paul. This we did. Then those on the outer circle were to start shadow boxing and to yell as loudly as we could, "Hit him!

Hit him!" This we also did. In about two minutes, the desired results occurred. Three teachers came running out of the building toward our circle, waving paddles as they ran.

If you had been one of the teachers, what would you have assumed you'd find in the middle of that circle of boys? We can't be certain what went through their minds, but I have a strong feeling that they thought they would find two boys engaged in a fist fight and that the crowd had gathered to watch and cheer for their friends.

As the teachers reached the edge of the crowd, they began pushing us aside while we continued to yell, "Hit him!" When they had cleared their way toward the center of the circle, they found Jimmy and Paul down on their hands and knees. Was the battle over? No, but the teachers seemed to be upset or maybe just embarrassed as they turned, without saying a word to any of us, and made their way back toward the school building. You see, Jimmy and Paul were not fighting at all but were involved in a friendly little game of marbles.

I've thought a lot about that experience over the years. While I am not proud that I was involved in that prank, I did learn a valuable lesson from it. You see, I realized that if Jimmy could deceive three teachers, all college graduates, while he was still in junior high, it is feasible that Satan could deceive even the very elect in his almost six thousand years of experience with deception.

One of the most frightening things about deception is that when people are being deceived, they do not know it is happening. To be deceived is to believe something that is not true. The fact that so few of us have any fear of being deceived seems in itself evidence of the overwhelming success Satan is having. When was the last time we asked ourselves in what areas we are being deceived, or when was the last time that we asked our Heavenly Father in prayer to please point out the areas in which we are being deceived? Most of us seem to feel that deceit is what happens to the other guy—the one who just isn't quite as wise as we are.

The scriptures are full of warnings about the deception

that will occur in the last days and the effectiveness of Satan's efforts. Nephi warns: "They have all gone astray save it be a few, who are the humble followers of Christ; nevertheless, they are led, that in many instances they do err because they are taught by the precepts of men." (2 Nephi 28:14.)

How is it possible for so many people in the latter days to go astray, including some followers of Christ? What methods is the adversary using to accomplish this? How are we being taught by the precepts of men?

For most of my life, I thought that that scripture applied to others and that it had nothing to do with Latter-day Saints. All that complacency disappeared when I read a statement by President John Taylor that pointed out a new possibility I hadn't considered before. He said:

> We are told that "Many will say to me in that day, Lord, Lord, have we not prophesied in Thy name and in Thy name have cast out devils, and in Thy name done many wonderful works?" Yet to all such he will say: "Depart from me, ye that work iniquity." You say that means the outsiders? No, it does not. Do they do many wonderful works in the name of Jesus? No....This means you, Latter-day Saints, who heal the sick, cast out devils and do many wonderful things in the name of Jesus.... Hear it, ye Latter-day Saints![1]

When I first read this statement I wondered how this could be. Surely active members of the Church cannot be deceived by Satan. Not me, anyway. Then I thought of some experiences, like the marble game, that helped me realize that it was possible the adversary could deceive even some Latter-day Saints, if we are not extremely careful.

One such experience happened to me in 1975. I had just graduated from Brigham Young University and had taken a job with a large business products company. Part of the training included a three-week workshop in Saint Paul, Minnesota. My wife had just delivered our second child, so she and our two young sons stayed behind in Texas.

One Saturday afternoon several of the new employees and I became bored just sitting around the hotel. We decided to go to the Minnesota State Fair. We had a nice time looking at the exhibits, and it helped take our minds off being homesick. After several hours we decided that we had seen enough and began making our way to the exit gate. Just before we reached the gate we stopped to observe a few people at an age-guessing booth. I was impressed that the man in the booth guessed the ages of two women to the exact year. I had my own guess of their ages and had miscalculated badly. I was now interested in this man and wondered how he had guessed the ages of the two women—and if he could guess my age. I was twenty-six at the time and was always being told that I looked about seventeen. Another man in our group, Reynard, also looked like a teenager, even though he was twenty-seven. We all decided to sign Reynard up to see how good a guesser the man really was.

According to the rules, if the man guessed an age within a year of the correct age, he won. If he missed, the challenger was the winner and received a prize. We paid the entry fee of one dollar, and Reynard wrote his correct age on a card for the assistant in the booth. The man looked closely at Reynard and wrote his guess on a card. We were excited because we knew he would miss the correct age by several years. The assistant turned over the card on which Reynard had put his correct age, twenty-seven, and showed it to the crowd gathered to watch. Then she turned over the card of the man in the booth. He had guessed Reynard's age as eighteen. We were all ecstatic. He had missed the correct age by nine years! I remember thinking as we walked away, "Boy, did we ever fool him—and he thought he was so smart." We laughed all the way to the front gate. Then we noticed the prize we had just won, and as suddenly as the laughing had begun, it stopped. The prize was a small plastic toy that had probably cost about ten cents. What a shock to think that we had just paid one dollar for a ten-cent prize! I then realized that the people in the booth didn't really care if they actually guessed an age correctly or not. If they guessed it correctly, they made a profit of one dollar; if they missed, they made a profit of ninety cents.

It was not the people at the booth who were fooled, but we ourselves. It was a humiliating experience for us all.

This experience is not so different from what Satan is trying to do. He makes things look so inviting that many people just can't resist giving them a try. I found out that day at the age booth that even active Latter-day Saints with temple marriages and college degrees can be easily deceived. If a group of college graduates can fall for the age-guessing trick, is it possible that Satan can present temptations so attractive that they will be hard to turn down, with far greater consequences than losing a dollar?

When I was younger, I thought that if I went to church every Sunday, married in the temple, and paid a full tithing, I would never have to worry about being led astray. I now realize the great danger of this philosophy. We must always be alert to the temptations and deceit, no matter who we are. Nephi warned us against such a misconception when he said, "And others will he pacify, and lull them away into carnal security, that they will say: All is well in Zion; yea, Zion prospereth, all is well—and thus the devil cheateth their souls, and leadeth them away carefully down to hell.... Therefore, wo be unto him that is at ease in Zion!" (2 Nephi 28:21, 24.)

But even with this very direct and plain warning, many continue to believe as I once did, that as long as we go to church, we no longer need to worry about Satan's deceptive devices. Perhaps Joseph Smith's revision of Matthew 24:24 will help us become even more fully aware of the dangers of this false assumption. It reads: "For in those days there shall also arise false Christs, and false prophets, and shall show great signs and wonders, insomuch that, if possible, they shall deceive the very elect, *who are the elect according to the covenant.*" (JS–M 1:22. Italics added.)

This scripture should leave no doubt in our minds as to the danger we face, even as members of the Church. But who are these false Christs and false prophets who will come in the last days? I think most of us have assumed over the years that they must be the leaders of false organized religions and cults. But do false prophets need to be members of organized churches? If so, it makes our job easy to avoid them. However, if these fraudulent teachers come from areas other than organized religions, they will be much harder to detect.

While I do not know who these false prophets are, I do know that on very few occasions have I ever witnessed an adult who was elect "according to the covenant" led away by any TV evangelist or leader of a religious cult or even another established religion. And yet I have seen far too many led away by the temptations of the world. Our real temptations seem to come from immorality, pride, pleasure seeking, riches, and other things of the world. Seldom do we lose to another religion a young person who is active in our church, but we have lost many to Word of Wisdom violations and immorality in its various forms. The forces of evil can make these things look so enticing that even some of the "elect" can't resist the temptations.

Who are these counterfeit prophets who are leading so many away from the truth? And what techniques are being used to mislead the people in our day, especially our youth? President Spencer W. Kimball gave us clues on where to look when he gave this wise counsel concerning sin: "Whoever said that sin was not fun? Whoever claimed that Lucifer was not handsome, persuasive, easy, friendly? Whoever said that sin was unattractive, undesirable, or nauseating in its acceptance? Transgression wears elegant gowns and sparkling apparel. It is highly perfumed, has attractive features, a soft voice."[2]

One day I presented a seminary lesson on the subject of deception. To demonstrate this statement by President Kimball, I brought to class a beautifully wrapped present. To make it even more appealing, I used a hundred-dollar bill for the bow. At the beginning of class, I stepped out into the hall and made a few adjustments to the present. Then I asked the students how many of them were interested in receiving the gift, which I held before them. I told them that inside the gift wrapping was a very useful item, that there was nothing inappropriate about it, and that I was sure their parents would not mind if they were to bring it home. The students' reaction was predictable. Not only did every one of the sixteen students want the present, but several started grabbing for it. I almost had to threaten a few to get them to sit down and stop trying to take it away from me.

I finally singled out one student and asked, "Diane, do you want this present?"

"You know I want it," she replied.

I reminded her that she didn't even know what was in the package.

"I don't care what's on the inside," she said. "I want that present!"

I'm sure Diane's desire was increased greatly by the hundred-dollar bill being used for the bow. I again asked, "Are you sure you want this present?"

"Yes, I do," she replied.

I told her to come to the front of the class and get it. Just as she reached up to take the small package, she let out a loud scream, as did several others in the class. The reason for the uproar was that inside the gift wrapping was a large and very powerful rat trap. When I had stepped out into the hall, I had cocked the trap and had kept my fingers on it until just before her hand came near it. When I let go, the wrapping paper was ripped apart and the loud noise from the released trap startled the whole class, especially Diane.

I had a very attentive class as we discussed how Satan tries his deception on us. He makes things that are very dangerous look so enticing that even good people sometimes fall for his lies. Alcoholic beverages, for example, are responsible for many problems in America, and yet the percentage of people who drink is increasing.

While doing some family-history research, I ran across some poems that were written by one of my relatives. I was very interested to find out more about him, since I had never met him. I learned that Billy had died a few years ago after spending the last years of his life totally alone, as a hopeless alcoholic. Although his father had been a branch president and his mother a Relief Society president, Billy rebelled as a teenager and began to associate with people who didn't have Church standards. He began to drink and steal and then dropped out of school at a young age. He became interested in boxing and eventually spent time as a professional in this sport. He married, but his life-style produced a strain on the relationship. The birth of a daughter brought new hope to Billy, and for a while he straightened his life out. But the pressures of life soon became more difficult and his drinking continued. Jobs were scarce, especially for someone with a drinking problem and no training or skills. This produced a terrible strain on his marriage, and his wife finally left him, taking his precious daughter with her. Billy's life was very lonely from that day forward. He lived his later years in a small apartment with no friends and no one to take care of him, and finally he died of the health problems related to his alcoholism.

Recently I found a poem, titled "I Remember You," that he wrote to his daughter during the last years of his life. It's a pitiful reminder of the consequences of following the deceits of the world.

> It was a long time ago when I kissed you goodbye—
> Yes, I let you go, but I'll never know why.
> You waved a farewell as you went through the door,
> And I never once dreamed that I'd see you no more.
>
> Your sweet baby picture is all that I own
> To remind me that maybe someday you'll come home.
> The little pink pillow that cradled your head,
> And your little rag that sat on your bed,
> Have been carefully wrapped and placed softly away,
> Just waiting for you to come home some day.
>
> How I miss your gay laughter and your sweet baby touch.
> If I only had known that I'd miss you so much
> Things might have been different in more ways than one.
> I'm the person who knows what your leaving has done.
>
> Your picture has faded, through the years it has worn
> Like this rum-sodden heart that's all tattered and torn.

But I gaze at it still, with a tear in my eye,
For it's all that I have to remember you by.

Lucifer has a way of making things appear very different from what they actually are. Many in our society are falling for his most malignant vices because of the enticing way they are presented. Many temptations lie concealed from view, but sometimes we see a thing so often that we overlook the obvious, even though it may pose an extreme danger to both ourselves and our families.

Try this experiment. Count all the F's as you read the following sentence:
FINISHED FILES ARE THE RESULT OF YEARS OF SCIENTIFIC STUDY COMBINED WITH THE EXPERIENCE OF MANY YEARS. How many did you find? I came up with three the first time I read the sentence, although the correct answer is six. Most people overlook the three *of*'s, even though they are right before our eyes and the sentence is not meant to be tricky.

Satan's desire to deliver us down to wickedness is no less intense than the Savior's desire to bring us to eternal life. Satan is trained, he has experience, and he has become very efficient and increasingly determined. We must be careful to examine our lives very carefully and realize whom we are up against.

If our families are to make it safely through the trying times associated with the last days, we must be constantly alert. Installing burglar alarms, dead-bolt locks, and window bars is futile in barring Satan from our homes. These devices are effective when used for the purpose for which they were designed, but it takes more than a dead-bolt lock to stop the dangers we are discussing here. Only through careful planning and Heavenly Father's help can our families find protection.

NOTES

1. Hyrum M. Smith and Janne M. Sjodahl, *Doctrine and Covenants Commentary* (Salt Lake City: Deseret Book, 1965), pp. 462-63.

2. Edward L. Kimball, ed., *The Teachings of Spencer W. Kimball* (Salt Lake City: Bookcraft, 1982), p. 152.

CHAPTER 3

HEROES AND PEER PRESSURE

About twenty young adults and I recently enjoyed an activity in Dallas, Texas, at a water amusement park that had swimming pools, water slides, wave pools, and various other water attractions.

We were all having lots of fun, when someone suggested we go down the dreaded "black hole." This ride was an enclosed tube about six stories high in which you twisted and turned in every conceivable way in darkness until you finally shot out the end, at a high rate of speed, into a pool of water. I assured the person who made the suggestion that I was doing just fine without going down this tube. But when someone else accused me of being "chicken," I had no choice but to ride down the "black hole." It turned out to be as bad as I had envisioned it. I was completely disoriented while going down, and my head was spinning badly by the time I hit the shallow pool of water at the bottom. But at least I couldn't be called a chicken, and I felt good about that.

A few minutes later we were joined by another group of young adults. Among this group was an energetic young returned missionary, Benny. After some small talk, Benny came up with a frightening suggestion — at least it was scary to me! He said, "You know what would be totally awesome? To go down the black hole backwards!" I exclaimed, "That ride is terrible going down frontwards! Why would any normal person want to go down backwards?" Some of the group agreed, but another member of the group, Danny, said, "Let's go for it — it WILL be awesome!"

With that remark, like a bunch of sheep, we followed Benny and Danny up the stairs to the top of the "black hole." As we waited for our turns, Benny turned to me and asked if I was going down backwards. I replied, "Why don't all of you guys go first and show me how it's done." All of the group in front of me went down the tube backwards, and with them went the pressure to give in, for fear of being laughed at. My guess was that they would be so dizzy at the end of the ride that they would never notice that I was going to come down frontwards.

Then, to my surprise, Angie, the young woman behind me, asked if I was going backwards. Chuckling, I said, "No. I am going frontwards. The guys will never know the difference." Then she said, "I can't believe it. Randal's a chicken! Even I am going down backwards!" Well, that's all it took. I wasn't going to have anyone laughing at me and calling me a chicken for being afraid. So I went down backwards — and, as I expected, I hated every minute of it. By the time I reached the bottom I couldn't tell whether I was going frontwards, backwards, or sideways, I was so disoriented.

The consequences of our actions came immediately. I staggered over to some chairs after the ride and sat down. Benny was sitting down on the grass looking about the same color as his green surroundings, while Danny leaned against a fence post and moaned with discomfort. Several of us felt ill for the rest of the day. And to my amusement, Benny and Danny were the sickest of all.

I've done a lot of thinking since that event and have decided that the process we were involved in that day is closely related to the techniques the adversary uses to ensnare us in sin.

Luckily for our group, going down the "black hole" backwards was not a sin. But the process that was used to get us to do it is similar to the one that Satan uses. The process goes something like this: Someone does something wrong. He tells his friends it was "totally awesome." If the friends don't do it also, others will laugh and call them "chicken," a "goody-goody," or a similar name. Finally they give in. Once these friends try the forbidden, they use the same methods to talk others into doing the same thing. And, like the young adults' experience with the "black hole," most victims do not think of the consequences of their actions until it is too late. Sometimes it takes years to see the effects of smoking, drinking, immorality, and other sins in a person's life.

If our families are to survive safely in today's world, we must be able to recognize the methods Satan uses and find ways to counter them. We should also realize that the people whom these methods affect most is our youth.

Before the school year started a couple of years ago, our family held a council to discuss our budget and determine what school clothes needed to be purchased for the year.

Our two sons in middle school said they each needed a few more pairs of blue jeans. When I asked them what brand name they felt we should buy, the immediate reply from both was Levi 501's. I then asked them why they wanted that specific brand, since the price was almost double that of some of the plain-pocket jeans. They replied in near unison, "Because they're the best."

I asked my wife, Wendy, to bring me a pair of Levi 501's and a pair of plain-pocket jeans out of my own drawer. I took one pants leg of each pair and turned the legs so that the overlapping stitching of both was showing, and then covered the upper part of the jeans with a towel. Then I asked the boys to tell me which pants leg was that of the Levi 501's. They looked for a long time, not wanting to make a mistake. Finally they admitted that they didn't know one from the other. I pointed out both pairs of jeans were made out of similar denim material; and except for a little thread on the pockets of one, there really didn't seem to be enough difference to justify the significant price differential.

Then the plea came that I had expected. Nathan, our oldest, said with a quivering voice, "Please, Dad, don't make us wear 'plain pockets' to school. Everyone will laugh at us if we do." I had to agree with him. It was probably true; many of the kids at their school would laugh at them. Of course, not all would; but the pacesetters of the school would probably look down on them for not wearing clothes accepted as being stylish and cool.

We had a long discussion that night about peer pressure and why we let others determine how we dress and even sometimes how we act. The boys didn't know all the answers, but they did agree that the pacesetters at school have an influence on many things, including dress, hairstyles, and choices of music and movies. I then asked my boys, "Where do you draw the line on their influence? What if they laugh at you for being honest in your schoolwork or for not participating in smoking, using drugs or alcohol, or indulging in premarital sex? Will you give in because they laugh at you or call you chicken?" Both replied they would not be influenced in those areas, but they again implored, "Please, Dad, don't make us wear plain-pocket jeans to school."

What should we have done? After a lengthy discussion, we did buy them Levi 501's to wear to school. As a family we decided that they really couldn't be very good missionaries for the Church if they were being laughed at and ridiculed because of the way they were dressed. But we have had several long talks since then about their feelings of fear, the impact of the media and advertising on our lives, and where to draw the line with the influence others will have on us.

To illustrate the power of peer pressure, I decided to see if other young people had been similarly affected by peers who all wore the same type of blue jeans to school. I called ten boys, ranging in age from middle school through high school, and asked them if they wanted to make a little money. They all said they did, but they wanted to know what the catch was. I told them I would give them each ten dollars to wear a pair of plain-pocket blue jeans to school for one day. The only catch was that if anyone asked, they had to say they were wearing the jeans because they liked them. Eight of the ten would not wear the jeans even though I kept increasing the amount I would give them. Several refused fifty dollars, and two even refused one hundred dollars. One said, "I won't do it for any price!"

When I asked the boys why they wouldn't take the challenge, they each said, "Because everyone will laugh at me if I do!"

Finally our stake president's son, Dan (who owed me ten dollars anyway), agreed to do it. The deal was that he could pay off his debt and, at the same time, help to prove a point about peer pressure. He would wear the plain pocket jeans for one day, but he couldn't tell anyone (at least not until the next day) why he was doing it. That night I bought him a pair of jeans at a local bargain store and took them to seminary the next morning. Here is the report he wrote on his day's experience:

> I was hoping the pants wouldn't fit or something else would happen, so everyone would know it was just a joke. All my confidence was replaced with fear as I stepped out of the car and noticed the stares of the cheerleaders, who were standing next to the school entrance. I thought I saw them giggling at me, but I couldn't be sure.
>
> As I walked down the hall to my first-period class, I heard someone yell behind me, "Hey, I *love* those pants!" When I walked into choir, about ten people burst into laughter. "Why did you wear those?" they asked, pointing at my pants. I answered, "Because I like them." The rest of the day went on in much the same way, with everyone laughing at me. This has been a real eye opener for me concerning the power of peer pressure. It's an experience that I don't care to repeat! At the end of the day, I asked myself the following questions:
>
> 1. How would it be to have to wear this brand of pants all the time?

2. How can the brand of pants change the public's opinion of your personality or character?

3. Do the looks I give people have the same effect on them that everyone's did on me that day?

4. I am a high school senior, president of the Madrigal Singers, president of the debate society, member of the student council, and I just won the grand prize in our school talent show. I wonder if I would have received these honors had I worn this brand of blue jeans every day?

Why do you think certain things are accepted by the young people in our schools and neighborhoods? Who sets the trends these young people are following? Why would anyone laugh and mock those who choose not to follow the crowd? Who are the pacesetters of our society that our young people admire, and what influence are they having on their lives?

Let's look first at the pacesetters or heroes on the national level, and maybe this will help explain, in part, what is happening on the local scene.

Determining who young people look up to becomes critical if we realize that people often imitate those whom they admire—the heroes in their lives. This is especially true of impressionable youth; they often try to imitate popular or well-known people in their own day-to-day living.

In a nationwide survey of teenagers, one researcher found that the first nine names listed as heroes were either movie and television personalities or rock musicians. Professional athletes appeared farther down the list. Dr. John Caughey, a University of Maryland anthropologist, explains:

> Imaginary social relationships pervade our lives. We spend at least as much time with imaginary relationships as in actual interactions with people. Many of these imaginary relationships are formed with celebrities because in our society we spend so much time consuming the media. The figures we encounter in the media invade our consciousness in such a way that it is impossible to grow up without being affected by them, even though we have never met them.
>
> The media world is fantastically attractive compared to real lives in which relationships may not be satisfying or

stable. Media relationships are with people who are, almost by definition, famous, successful, dynamic and good looking. Celebrities have become the gods of our social system because our success-oriented culture has placed them at the top.[1]

Are LDS teens much different in their views of those they most admire from teenagers in the national polls? After several surveys, I have been a little shocked and dismayed to find that results of the LDS teens surveyed match, almost exactly, the youth in the national polls. Young people both in and out of the Church, with some exceptions, are consistent in looking up to three main groups of people as their heroes: movie and television stars, rock musicians, and professional athletes. And all of these groups share a common factor—they have all been created by the media! I'm convinced that there are some teenagers, both in and out of the Church, whose heroes don't fit into one of these three categories. But equally convincing is the large number that are looking to these three groups as persons to admire and pattern their lives and way of thinking after.

In most cases, Satan uses people on earth to carry out his work. If he could corrupt any group of people, whom would it be? It seems logical that if he could go for any group, it would be the very people so many look up to and admire. That way he gets not only those individuals but also the huge number who follow their examples.

How can we find out who our children's heroes are? A good place to start would be their bedrooms. Are there posters on the walls? Ask your children, in a spirit of love, to explain about the people or things pictured on the posters and why they have chosen to look at these pictures every day. Ask them to show you their record albums and to tell you about the songs on them and the soloists or groups that sing them. Ask them about their favorite TV and movie stars and why they are impressed with them.

Now let's look a little closer at the people who seem to be at the top of almost every poll. Why are these persons at the top of the heroes list of our teenagers? What influence are they having on our young people and on society in general? What do they, as a whole and not individually, think or feel about the following areas: premarital sex? divorce? living together unmarried? tobacco? liquor? cocaine? illegitimate births? extravagance in clothes, cars, homes, or jewelry?

Unfortunately, several studies have shown that among these particular groups, there is an extremely high amount of participation in these activities.

Now, let's look at these "heroes" again with some different topics. How might these people (again, as a whole and not as individuals) feel about someone who prays regularly? reads the scriptures? attends church regularly? is morally clean? lives the Word of Wisdom to its fullest?

Would they be very impressed, somewhat impressed, or not impressed at all? If these persons, pacesetters of our society, are being looked up to and imitated, then the answers to these questions become extremely important to our families, since these are the very things we are trying to teach. Let's examine the use of profanity, as an example.

Recently I asked my nephew Cory, a sophomore in high school, to count the profane words he heard at school in one day. That evening he called and asked me over to his house to look at his profanity count. I soon found he had gone a little further than I had asked. He not only counted the number of profane words he heard that day, but he also had listed the first letter of each word on paper and then put them in order by the actual number of times each word was used. Although he didn't count before school, during lunch, or after school, his total came to 194 profane words used in the classrooms during the day!

The next day, I had to stand in line for an hour and fifteen minutes to pick up some basketball tickets at the university where I teach. I did a similar profanity count while in line. I counted 115 profane words used by those standing around me. It was interesting that the top three words on my list were the same three as on my nephew's list.

Next, I wanted to try to find out if there was a relationship between our lists and the words celebrities were using in the media. I asked ten regular moviegoers what they felt were the two profane words used most often in the current movies they had seen. All ten told what they thought were the first and second words used most often by giving me the first letter. All ten listed the same word as number one, and that word was the same one as had appeared on both my nephew's list and my own personal list. And eight out of the ten moviegoers named as the second most commonly used profane word the same word as on my other lists!

Several students found out about my study and began bringing profanity counts from movies and from the different schools they attended. Overall, the results were the same.

One student even brought me a detailed count from a cassette tape of a popular comedian. In the tape, over four hundred profane words were used—and the two most frequently used words were the same two as on my other lists. This entertainer had just been voted in one poll as the number-one hero of young Americans between the ages thirteen and eighteen. And in a poll at our local university, he received twice as many votes as all other entertainers combined as the person students most wanted to see brought to campus for a performance.

The student who gave me the information from this cassette added this comment on his paper: "As I listened to the comedian's tape, extracting the profanity, I found it was very easy to find them at first. But as I got more into the tape, I found myself listening to the stories he was telling, often thinking them very funny, although they were very vulgar. Several times I had to rewind the tape to see if he had said a bad word or not!"

Later, while reading a national newspaper one day, I noted a study on profanity done by a professor at North Adams State College in Massachusetts. I called him and he sent me a study he had just completed in the eastern United States. At the top of his list were the same two words as on all the other lists I had collected. I wondered how it could be that of all the hundreds of possible four-letter words that could be used, the lists in Massachusetts, Southeast Texas, and the surveyed movies all had the same top two.

Now comes an interesting question. Did these celebrities come to both Texas and Massachusetts to ask teenagers which profane words they liked the most so they could include them in their movies or comedy acts, or have the young people not only in Texas and Massachusetts, possibly in our whole society, come to speak certain words because the people whom they admire use them? Although the relationship seems to be a definite possibility, it is hard to prove. I do feel, however, that there is enough evidence that we should consider the possibility of a link.

During the last few years there has been a tremendous increase in the use of snuff, or smokeless tobacco, among teenage boys, particularly football and baseball players, and cowboys. The amount of smokeless tobacco sold annually in the United States has increased 60 percent in recent years. And while national figures on teenage use are not available, local surveys suggest that between 20 percent and 40 percent of all high school boys are now dipping. In Texas, 55 percent of all young dippers started before age thirteen. This is happening despite the warnings that the nicotine level in the blood is higher in smokeless tobacco users than in cigarette smokers.

To what might we attribute this dramatic increase? Why do football and baseball players and cowboys have the highest rates of use? And why boys and not girls? Perhaps one reason is that teenage boys have been inspired by TV commercials and other media advertisements featuring well-known sports stars, including a professional baseball player, a former professional football player, and a professional rodeo star.

Another example comes from one of the largest manufacturers of athletic shoes in the United States. This company pays a well-known professional basketball player one million dollars a year to appear in ads for the company's shoes. Does this strategy work? Are young people influenced to buy these products? Look around to see which shoes sell the best. Why? The answer seems obvious. Many teenagers buy certain brands of shoes because a star athlete wears them and they want to be like their hero, and not necessarily because these particular shoes are the best for the money.

If heroes, pacesetters, celebrities, or whatever we choose to call them, can sell shoes and smokeless tobacco to young people, can they also sell their moral values and life-styles by their examples? The evidence suggests that this is the case.

On a local level, young people have pacesetters in their schools and neighborhoods. Who are the popular teenagers at your schools? Are they the horn players in the band, members of the yearbook staff, the future farmers, the athletes, the cheerleaders, the library staff? The responses may vary somewhat from area to area, but many times we find that the life-styles and beliefs of the local pacesetters come very close to those of the national pacesetters whom they admire. Many young people see nothing wrong with drinking, occasional drug use, or premarital sex. Material things, such as expensive and stylish clothes, keeping up with the latest fads, fancy cars, expensive stereos, large record collections, and the freedom to go and come as they please seem to add to the popularity of youths in many areas. This influence is often referred to as peer pressure. Although it can take many forms, one of the most common and most effective methods used is mocking. In the Book of Mormon, Alma clearly warns us against its use: "And again I say unto you, is there one among you that doth make a mock of his brother, or that heapeth upon him persecutions? Wo unto such an one, for he is not prepared, and the time is at hand that he must repent or he cannot be saved." (Alma 5: 30-31.)

I know from my own experience that mocking is a powerful tool. When I was in the ninth grade, I was a bench warmer on our ward softball team. Most of the starters were seniors and helped make our team good enough that we advanced to the all-Church tournament in Salt Lake City. We had several extra practices that summer, trying to get ready for our trip. One day it was very hot, so I decided to wear shorts to practice. As I walked up, one of the star players whistled at me and yelled across the field, "Hey, everybody, look at bird legs!" I turned around and walked home, feeling about two inches high, and changed into some long pants. Since that day, some twenty-three years ago, I have never liked to wear short pants or even a swimsuit. The strange thing is that I don't have skinny legs at all and I know it, but I still feel self-conscious. Mocking is a powerful tool!

On another occasion I was the unknowing mocker. I still feel bad about it, but the worst thing about mockery is that it is nearly impossible to undo the damage it causes. When I was in high school, my sister's fiancé came to visit our home wearing some new pants. These particular pants were the latest fashion, but I said, "Hey, did your daddy let you wear his pants today?" I thought it was a fairly funny comment, although I don't remember his laughing much. Later my sister told me that he had just purchased those pants and it was the first time he had worn them. After that evening, he never wore them again.

When I was about ten, I leaned over to my mother as she was singing the opening song in church and said, "Momma, you need singing lessons!" Twenty-eight years later, my mother still doesn't like to sing, and guess whom she blames? I have tried many times to get her to believe I was only joking and that she really does have a nice singing voice, but nothing I have said has restored her confidence.

Yes, mocking is a powerful tool, and few can withstand its power without giving in.

It is for this reason that Lehi's vision of the tree of life becomes so frightening. He says that he saw people grasping hold of the rod of iron, pressing forward to partake of the fruit of the tree. Then he saw something that made him exceedingly fearful:

> After they had partaken of the fruit of the tree they did cast their eyes about as if they were ashamed. And I also cast my eyes round about, and beheld, on the other side of

the river of water, a great and spacious building; and it stood as it were in the air, high above the earth. And it was filled with people, both old and young, both male and female; and their manner of dress was exceedingly fine; and they were in the attitude of mocking and pointing their fingers towards those who had come at and were partaking of the fruit. And after they had tasted of the fruit they were ashamed, because of those that were scoffing at them; and they fell away into forbidden paths and were lost. (1 Nephi 8:25-28.)

Although the people in his dream were both old and young, both male and female, they had a few things in common. What were they? Lehi says that "their manner of dress was exceedingly fine," which apparently describes people who were being looked up to, people who were probably pacesetters. Lehi also said they were "in the attitude of mocking and pointing their fingers at those who were partaking of the fruit." And then we come to the most frightening part of the dream. Obviously those who had progressed along the rod of iron (word of God) until they had actually partaken of the fruit (love of God) were good people and possibly even active church members; yet Lehi says, "And after they had tasted of the fruit they were ashamed, because of those that were scoffing at them, and they fell away into forbidden paths and were lost." They must have had some respect for those who mocked them, or why would they have given in?

As I have taught and observed the young people of the Church, I have witnessed this same powerful tool being used over and over on them. Some are strong enough to endure and overcome adverse pressure by their peers, but others receive the same kind of mockery and scoffing and fall away into forbidden paths and are lost. There seems to be at least some correlation between those who have worldly heroes and those who fall away.

In our families we must help our children develop their self-esteem so they can withstand this kind of pressure. We must expose them to real heroes, such as Jesus Christ, Moses, Nephi, Alma, Ruth, Naomi, Moroni, Joseph Smith, Ezra Taft Benson, and others. If we don't expose our families to such examples in our homes, it is doubtful they will ever think of them as heroes and people to follow.

There is apparently a direct correlation between the amount of exposure we receive to something and our attitude toward it. For instance, if we are constantly exposed to classical music, we will probably like classical music and look up to the great composers. If we are constantly exposed to the national average of approximately twenty-eight hours of TV per week, we will probably admire and look up to TV stars. And I'm confident that if we are exposed to the scriptures and church history for large portions of time, we will choose prophets and church leaders as the people we look to for our examples. In our homes, who receives the most exposure—righteous heroes or worldly heroes?

Somehow we must find the strength to stand against the tremendous odds Lehi described as the large and spacious building, or the world. President Ezra Taft Benson has given us this counsel: "Most of these heroes who are being glamorized today are no longer noble, accomplished, humble, or righteous. From reports in books, magazines, and newspapers—especially the youth sections—we learn that they are lewd, obscene, immoral, avaricious, and in some cases even cruel. It is the very life-style we are here to avoid that is paraded before our young people by their celebrated peers. To deflect the admiration of youth from these examples of the ugly life, we must start young."[2]

Recently our family visited the San Jacinto battlefield and monument where Texas won its independence from Mexico. As we walked through the museum on the site, my eye caught an old tattered flag. It had scorched spots on the corners, and the "Lone Star" appeared very dingy. The caption under the flag read "This is the flag that flew at the Battle of the Alamo." Although the flag was a replica, a chill went through me as I thought of that event and the heroes who fought there for their lives and for liberty. Encased in glass beside the flag was a letter from Colonel William Travis, the commander of the 182 men who fought and died for Texas and its independence. The letter, a plea for help addressed "to the people of Texas and all Americans in the world," read:

> Fellow citizens and compatriots—I am besieged, by a thousand or more of the Mexicans under Santa Anna—I have sustained a continual bombardment and cannonade for 24 hours and have not lost a man. The enemy has demanded a surrender at discretion, otherwise the garrison are to be put to the sword, if the fort is taken—I have answered the demand with a cannon shot, and our flag still waves proudly from the walls. I shall never surrender or retreat. Then, I call on you in the name of Liberty, of patriotism and everything dear to the American character, come to our aid, with all dispatch. The enemy is receiving reinforcements daily and will no doubt increase to three or four thousand in four or five days. If this call is neglected, I am determined to sustain myself as long as possible and die like a soldier who never forgets what is due to his honor and that of his country—*Victory or Death.*

Colonel Travis underlined the last three words three times. A short time later, he and all his men gave their lives for their cause, rather than surrender to the enemy.

As our families face the tremendous forces of evil in these last days, and we face wickedness, mocking, and scorn on every side from the people of the "large and spacious building," may we too answer with cannon fire—the cannon fire of courage to say, "I shall never surrender or retreat to evil, no matter what the odds! Victory over evil, or death!"

NOTES

1. "Fantasy Friends Fill a Gap in People's Lives," A Conversation with John Caughey, *U.S. News and World Report,* July 16, 1984, p. 106.

2. Ezra Taft Benson, *God, Family, Country: Our Three Great Loyalties* (Salt Lake City: Deseret Book, 1975), p. 250.

CHAPTER 4

THE MOST SUCCESSFUL SCHOOL SYSTEM

Have you ever wondered what the most successful school system in history has been? By school, I mean the process of teaching and learning, not a room or building. I believe that television is that most successful school system. While some may debate my nomination, I would challenge them to find a more successful one. With television, both teaching and learning are occurring. In fact, one of the most significant findings of research on TV viewing and its effects is that there is no significant difference between what students learn from TV and what they learn from face-to-face conventional teaching. In a way, that is very exciting, assuming that what is being taught will make us better people because of it. On the other hand, it is very frightening if the ideas being conveyed are false or in any way harmful.

To better understand the power and influence of television, let's think of all the programs offered on TV as independent study classes. Every time we turn on the TV set, let's imagine that we are actually attending a class. This shouldn't be hard to imagine, since in a very real sense this is, in fact, what we are doing. The actors and actresses in our illustration are our teachers, and the TV script writers are the authors of the textbooks that the teachers use. Following are just a few of the accomplishments of this gigantic and immensely successful institution, the TV school.

COMMUNITY INVOLVEMENT

The community involvement achieved by this school system has never been matched in American history, or, for that matter, in the history of the world. In fact, 98 percent of all men, women, and children in America are not only signed up for classes, but are actually attending on a regular basis. I challenge any other educational institution to match this feat. Over 100 million people will be attending class on any given night in the United States, with close to 230 million individuals taking classes at least on a part-time basis.

The time spent by Americans in this school, according to a 1987 Nielsen Report on Television, is staggering. Consider the hours Americans spend attending TV classes each week. For ages 18 through 34, men spend 23 hours and 54 minutes, while women spend 29 hours and 32 minutes. For ages 35 through 54, men watch TV 28 hours and 26 minutes, and women watch 32 hours and 34 minutes. Men 55 and over watch TV 39 hours and 14 minutes, and women watch 43 hours and 58 minutes.

Thus, the average American individual spends over 28 hours a week attending class, and this figure is rising yearly. Attendance in this school system ranks behind only sleep and work as a consumer of our time. Before a child reaches five years of age, he or she will already have spent more time attending television classes than the average student spends in the college classroom to get a four-year degree. In a one-year period, the average American will spend approximately 1,456 hours being instructed by the TV. By high school graduation, an average American child will have spent more than 11,000 hours in the public school and 22,000 hours in TV school, but only an estimated 1,200 hours in meaningful conversation with his or her parents.

DROPOUT RATE

Another astounding accomplishment of this school system is the dropout rate. It doesn't seem to matter at what age a student begins attending classes: once enrolled, most become so excited about education that they almost never drop out. There are no mandatory attendance laws in this school, and students are free to sign up for classes or to drop out at will, but most have a strong desire to stay.

CLASS TIMES

A unique feature of this school is the times classes are available. They are held 24 hours a day, 7 days a week, 365 days a year. The old saying "we never close" truly applies to this school. If you are interested in taking a class, the school will provide the teachers at any time of the day or night. No major school system has ever offered such a schedule.

CLASS RESTRICTIONS

There are no restrictions or prerequisites to any of the classes offered in this school. Anyone, from newborn child to teenager to senior citizen, can attend any class. Even whole families are encouraged to attend class together. The more students in a class, the better, as far as the school's administrators are concerned. Children are not restricted from attending even the many classes on adult subjects. Occasionally the administrators do point out that the subject of a class may be more appropriate for adults, but they usually don't bother because they have found most young people really enjoy attending adult classes.

DRESS CODES

There are no dress codes of any kind at this school. You

never have to worry about getting all dressed up to come to class unless you choose to. It's a "come as you are" type of learning environment, though there is a tendency for some students to try to dress and look like their favorite teachers.

CLASSES FOR EVERYONE

The TV school is the most completely integrated institution of learning in the history of education. People from all religions, nationalities, and races and all walks of life may attend. It is also interesting to note that the uneducated, those who have no desire to complete a public-school education, attend the school in extremely high numbers.

CHILD-CARE SERVICE

A tremendous service provided by the school system is child care. It is the largest child-care and babysitting service in the nation. The teachers will entertain your children 24 hours a day, 7 days a week, 365 days a year. Most parents feel that the biggest enticement for using it is that this service is provided free of charge, no matter how much you use it.

FREE TUITION

You are probably wondering by now what the tuition must be for a school that has so much to offer. Amazingly, the school has free tuition. All you need to do is purchase your own school materials, which come in a set and can be purchased at any appliance store. Who pays the bills? Surely there must be a tremendous cost involved to provide such a wide variety of classes and services. It's true that the cost of running the system is staggering. To pay the operating costs, the administrators solicit huge sums from business sponsors. In exchange, the school administrators allow the businesses to come into the classrooms to sell their products to the students. Because so many of the students buy their products, the businesses may pay up to $500,000 a minute to come into the classrooms and sell their wares.

THE MOST SUCCESSFUL SCHOOL SYSTEM 43

LIFE-STYLES OF THE TEACHERS

No schoolteachers have ever been paid such high salaries as those of the people teaching in the TV school system. It would be difficult to imagine any teachers who have ever had as much attention from their students as these now enjoy. In some cases millions flock to any given class just to see and listen to the teachers whom they admire so much. Maybe it is due to this excessive admiration and high salary structure that some of the teachers indulge in unbecoming behavior. Although there are many fine teachers in the system, there are also many who openly engage in sexual affairs, illegitimate births, abortions, cohabitation, homosexuality, alcohol abuse, pride, and vanity.

President Gordon B. Hinckley has shared the following information about the life-styles of those who write the texts upon which TV teachers base their teachings. Notice that he uses the words "educate us" in describing their influence:

> "A survey of influential television writers and executives in Hollywood has shown that they are far less religious than the general public and 'diverge sharply from traditional values' on such issues as abortion, homosexual rights and extramarital sex.... While nearly all of the 104 Hollywood professionals interviewed had a religious background, 45 percent now say they have no religion, and of the other 55 percent, only 7 percent say they attend a religious service as much as once a month.
>
> "This group has had a major role in shaping the shows whose themes and stars have become staples in our popular culture....
>
> "Eighty percent of the respondents said they did not regard homosexual relations as wrong, and 51 percent did not deem adultery as wrong. Of the 49 percent who called extramarital affairs wrong, only 17 percent felt that way strongly, the study said. Nearly all — 97 percent — favored the right of a woman to choose an abortion, 91 percent holding that view strongly. By contrast, other surveys have indicated that 85 percent of Americans consider adultery wrong, 71

percent regard homosexual activity wrong and nearly three-fourths of the public wants abortion limited to certain hard cases or banned altogether." (*Los Angeles Times*, 19 Feb. 1983, part 2, page 5.)

These are the people [TV script writers and executives] who, through the medium of entertainment, are educating us in the direction of their own standards, which in many cases are diametrically opposed to the standards of the gospel.[1]

CLASS OFFERINGS

The TV school offers a great variety of classes for its students. Hundreds of different classes and subjects are offered each year. Some acceptable family classes are offered if you look closely for them. Class offerings include such subjects as foreign affairs, history, current events, medicine, entertainment, sports, music, and the arts. Although most would agree that the school has been one of the most important things that has ever happened to education, many are concerned with some of the classes being offered.

While it is true that the school offers some positive, uplifting classes, it also offers many very degrading classes. Students can choose classes in rape, robbery, assault, burglary, arson, bombings, murder, suicide, dishonesty, vandalism, extortion, drugs, alcohol, gang warfare, illicit sex, and abortion. Many public-school officials and researchers contend that some of the students in the TV school actually demonstrate in society lessons that they learned in a TV class.

School officials claim that they are only giving students what they want and reflecting society's standards. Their opponents argue that the TV students are so interested in this type of education that they will attend classes no matter what is offered and that school administrations should offer more positive classes. The opponents also contend that many classes do not reflect society, but create society.

We could go on and on, but I hope the above illustration of viewing television as a school has been helpful. It has helped me on many occasions to control the programs (classes) that have been offered in our home as I realized that my family was being taught by what we viewed. As one writer has said, "The genres of TV combine to give us everything we always wanted in real life and could never have, everything we always wanted in real life, but were afraid to have, everything we used to have in real life, but lost. In doing this, they have actually become real life, influencing every action we take and every word we say."[2]

Television is one of the most remarkable and powerful inventions in history. Its potential for good is well documented. What a great privilege it is to watch general conference and the Tabernacle Choir, to see a man actually walk on the moon, to witness the inauguration of a president and to listen to his addresses and reports to the nation. How thrilling it is to watch a favorite sports team play in our own living room in living color and even to see a favorite play repeated through instant replays. How delightful it is to be entertained by some of the greatest musicians in America. How fortunate we are to see history in the making.

In many ways we would be very unfortunate to live in a world without the benefits of TV. In some ways it has been a great influence for good in our society. But because of the tremendous influence that it wields, we must be extremely careful of its use. President Ezra Taft Benson has warned: "The magnetism of TV and radio is in the accessibility of their mediocrity. Lovely is not an adjective to describe most of their products. The inventors of these wonders were inspired by the Lord. But once their good works were introduced to the world, the power of darkness began to employ them for our destruction. In each medium—the phonograph, motion pictures, radio, and television—the evolution of decline from the inventor's intentions can be easily traced."[3]

It is possible to trace the decline in American television from its original programs. As an example, a prime-time (7:00 to 10:00 P.M.) schedule check going back thirty years found that in 1955, no violent, crime-oriented programs were offered. By 1965, six hours of such programs were offered each week. By

1975, twenty-one hours of violent programs were being offered. By 1986, twenty-nine hours of violent programs were being offered.

Not only is violence increasing on TV, but every form of immorality, vice, and corruption is also being paraded before our family's eyes in ever-increasing amounts. Ask yourself if the same kinds of sexually related scenes and messages of all too many programs of today were found in the programs of twenty years ago. We are being exposed to growing amounts of inappropriate material if we choose to watch TV without being selective.

Recently I completed an extensive survey for a major broadcasting company on the content of television programming. My task was to monitor one week of prime-time television on all three major network stations. I recorded all three network programs for the week on VCR tape, a total of sixty-three hours of prime-time programming. This may seem like a lot of television time until you compare it with the 420 hours of programs actually shown that week on the three network affiliates in my area. My sample came only from prime time, and it did not include even one-sixth of the total programming offered that week on just the three major networks. Compared to the total programming of all the cable and satellite stations, my sample was actually extremely small.

In my research, I viewed the programs using a video recorder, so I could start and stop more easily all the scenes during the actual programming or in advertising that were predetermined to be appropriate or inappropriate behavior or messages. I was to look for twenty-six different behaviors and messages that were predetermined to be negative and twenty-six that were labeled positive. The list of negative behaviors included such things as murder, use of a deadly weapon, destruction, physical abuse, alcoholic beverage use, drug use, profanity, theft, and scenes or talk related to sex. On the positive side, I was looking for such things as stable families, expressions of love, family activities, patriotism, antidrinking messages, anti-illicit sex messages, and church attendance.

THE MOST SUCCESSFUL SCHOOL SYSTEM 47

As you might imagine, this research was a very painstaking project that took hundreds and hundreds of hours to complete. The end result was a report of almost four hundred pages titled *American Prime-Time*. Figures 1 through 4 are only a small sample of the things observed in this research project. I do not identify the individual networks by name, but only call them network 1, network 2, and network 3. The percentages listed refer to the total percent of prime-time programs presented by that network that had the listed behaviors or messages for the week of May 24 through May 30, 1986.

Figure 1
Sample Percentages of Social Problems in Prime-Time Programs

Network	Profanity	Deadly Weapons	Use of Alcohol	Property Destruction	Physical Abuse	Sexual Material
1	88	60	88	56	72	80
2	86	90	95	86	86	81
3	73	64	86	55	64	64

Figure 2
Sample of Combined Social Problems in Prime-Time Programs

Social Problem	Number of Instances or Scenes for Week	Total If Continued at This Rate for 1 Year
1. Deadly weapons	370 scenes*	19,240
2. Profanity	319 instances	16,588
3. Use of alcohol	228 scenes*	11,856
4. Sex-related material	188 scenes*	9,776
5. Property destruction	153 instances	7,956
6. Physical abuse	138 instances	7,176
7. Murder	30 instances	1,560

*Scenes mean the actual number is much higher, but it was impossible to identify actual numbers involved. For instance, the number of deadly weapons used in a large shoot-out could not be determined. Only the number of scenes was counted.

Figure 3
Percentage of Prime-Time Programs Containing Positive Aspects

Network	Expressions of Love	Physical Fitness	Stable Families	Anti-smoking	Family Activities
1	24	20	20	0	8
2	43	24	24	10	0
3	23	23	27	9	9

Note: None of the programs viewed promoted church attendance or sexual morality.

Figure 4
Sample of Combined Positive Aspects of Prime-Time Programs

Positive Aspects	Number of Instances or Scenes for Week	Total If Continued at This Rate for 1 Year
1. Expressions of love	31	1,612
2. Physical fitness	18	936
3. Stable families	14	728
4. Antismoking	5	260
5. Family activities	5	260
6. Anti-illicit sex message	0	0
7. Church attendance	0	0

The project turned out to be one of the most depressing experiences of my life. I wondered what had happened to the good, clean family programs I had watched as a youth, and I gained an even stronger testimony that we need to be very careful with our use of television. It can be a useful and positive tool if it is used properly, but it must be controlled closely.

Although many other points could be made, I believe enough evidence has been cited here to show that we have a challenge on our hands. The research also indicates that the problem is growing rapidly as the networks try to hold onto their audiences in the face of ever-increasing competition. If we as families are to survive, we must monitor not only the amount of TV shown in our homes, but also the types of programs that are allowed in our homes. Satan's main purpose is to try to destroy our families. If he can accomplish this, he will not only win the battle, but he will also win the war. Let us not allow his teachings to enter our homes by our own invitation. Remember the words of President Spencer W. Kimball:

> Again we see history repeating itself. When we see the pornography, the adulterous practices, homosexuality gone rampant, the looseness and permissiveness of an apparently increasing proportion of the people, we say the days of Satan have returned and history seems to repeat itself.
>
> When we see the depravity of numerous people of our own society in their determination to force upon people vulgar presentations, filthy communications, unnatural practices, we wonder, has Satan reached forth with his wicked, evil hand to pull into his forces the people of this earth? Do we not have enough good people left to stamp out the evil which threatens our world? Why do we continue to compromise with evil and why do we continue to tolerate sin?[4]

If we fail to monitor the influences that come into our homes, our families may be desensitized to sin in our own living rooms by our own invitation!

NOTES

1. Gordon B. Hinckley, "Be Not Deceived," *Ensign*, November 1983, pp. 45-46.

2. Edward Jay Whetmore, *Mediamerica: Form, Content, and Consequence of Mass Communication* (Belmont, California: Wadsworth Publishing Co., 1985), p. 194.

3. Ezra Taft Benson, *God, Family, Country* (Salt Lake City: Deseret Book, 1975), p. 250.

4. Spencer W. Kimball, "Why Do We Continue to Tolerate Sin?," *Ensign*, May 1975, p. 109.

CHAPTER 5

LEARNING TO CONTROL TELEVISION

One of the most enjoyable callings I have ever held in the Church was teaching a group of five-year-olds in Primary. In one class period these youngsters taught me more about the power of television than I had learned from years of studying the subject. Before that day I had always thought that TV influenced children out in the world, but that it didn't have that much effect in the homes of our Latter-day Saints because we would be able to counter its influence with the gospel. I have since changed my opinion, in part because of my Primary class.

As part of the lesson, we talked about the beautiful creations of the world and how powerful Heavenly Father and Jesus are to have been able to create so many wonderful things for us. To help reinforce this concept, I asked the children who they thought was the most powerful person in the universe. Almost in unison, the children answered, "He-Man!" Knowing that He-Man was a popular TV character, I first laughed at this response. But my laughter was soon replaced with concern when I saw that they were very serious. They really did believe this to be true.

I told the class that He-Man was not really the most powerful being in the universe, but that Heavenly Father and Jesus were. Some of the students seemed to believe me and some didn't, so I repeated some of the things I had said. Then I asked one of the boys, "Damon, who is the most powerful being in the universe, Heavenly Father and Jesus or He-Man?" He didn't hesitate. "He-Man can lift Heavenly Father and Jesus over his head with one hand!" Needless to say, I was shocked with this answer, and I soon learned that no matter what I said, he and a few of the other children would not change their opinion.

After class, I told Damon's father what had happened. That evening the father called to tell me he had talked to his son at length and had tried to convince him that He-Man was just pretend and that Heavenly Father and Jesus were the most powerful beings in the universe—but he wasn't sure he had changed Damon's opinion.

Later I thought about all the children who must hold a similar belief. Many of them do not have parents who try to teach them otherwise. Why would programs such as this one, even in fun, want to teach our children to believe false teachings such as this? Are we being influenced by the programs on television? If so, is the influence positive or negative? If you have a small child, ask him the same question I asked my Primary class. You may be surprised to learn how much influence television has had in your own home.

Television is perceived by most persons as a form of entertainment, but I believe it is much more than that. It is the only experience that almost everyone in our society has in common. TV not only shapes culture, it spreads culture. Let's look at a small sample of areas that may be affected.

HOW TV INFLUENCES VIEWERS

1. *Violence.* In polls conducted by Lou Harris, Americans were asked if they felt crime was a serious problem. In 1963, 2 percent of the respondents considered crime a major prob-

lem. By 1970, 70 percent considered it a major problem. And by 1983, the figure had risen to 81 percent. Why the drastic change of opinion in just twenty years? Could the deterioration in television programming be related to the change of opinion? How much crime and violence is shown on television? In 1954, 17 percent of prime-time programs contained violence. By 1961, the figure had risen to 60 percent, and by 1986, it was 80 percent.

It is estimated that by the time a child has graduated from high school, he will have witnessed some 150,000 violent episodes, including an estimated 25,000 deaths, on television. Does this bombardment of violence have an impact on its viewers? Many researchers studying the effect of the media say yes. Dr. Victor L. Cline, a Latter-day Saint who has written extensively on this subject, has said: "The hard scientific evidence clearly demonstrates that watching television or movie violence sometimes for only a few hours, and in some studies even for a few minutes, can and does instigate aggressive behavior that would not otherwise occur."[1]

On TV, few arguments or conflicts are ever settled without a fight. Violence is depicted as a way of life. From the evidence, it appears that some viewers may attempt to act out what they are viewing.

Is it a coincidence that the violence in our society is increasing at a rate similar to that shown on TV? Is it possible that society is being influenced by the constant barrage of violence being shown? Let's consider at a few examples, keeping in mind what has happened to television programming.

Have you ever wondered what the number one murder weapon used on television is? I found in my research that the handgun was by far the number one choice by criminals. What is the number one choice of real criminals in America? In 1985 handguns killed 48 people in Japan, 8 people in Great Britain, 34 people in Switzerland, 52 in Canada, 58 in Israel, 21 in Sweden, 42 in West Germany — and 10,728 in the United States.[2]

Other types of violent behavior in America have also risen dramatically, as these figures indicate:[3]

Aggravated Assault

Year	Number
1960	154,000
1970	335,000
1975	485,000
1980	673,000
1985	723,000

Rape

Year	Number
1960	17,200
1970	38,000
1975	56,100
1980	83,000
1985	87,300

Robbery

Year	Number
1960	108,000
1970	350,000
1975	465,000
1980	566,000
1985	498,000

Child Maltreatment

Year	Number
1960	N/A
1970	N/A
1976	669,000
1980	1,154,000
1984	1,727,000

The Apostle Paul counseled the saints in his day to "abstain from all appearance of evil." (1 Thessalonians 5:22.) How well do we keep this commandment if we apply it to television viewing? Would we allow our children to associate with a violent criminal in our own neighborhoods? If not, should we allow them to associate with such characters in our homes through violent television programs?

2. *Immorality.* One of the most pervasive problems I found in accumulating my TV research was that 75 percent of the programs had episodes of either actual or implied illicit sex. One family-planning group has estimated that in 1986, TV programs in America had 20,000 episodes of "suggested sexual relations." This cannot help but affect the attitudes of viewers, especially when the immorality is portrayed as desirable and usually with no negative consequences. While we do not know the exact relationship between the increase in sex on TV and the increase in immorality in our society, we do know that in 1986, the number of adolescent pregnancies was more than one million a year. The number of births to unmarried women

rose from 141,600 (3.9 percent of all births) in 1950 to 770,400 (21 percent of all births) in 1984. Add to that the fact that 1.5 million abortions are now being performed in the United States each year, and we can see that the problem is enormous.

Another area that has seen a dramatic increase is the number of unmarried persons living together. In 1970 the figure was estimated at 523,000 couples; by 1984 it had risen to an estimated 1.988 million.[4]

Is it only coincidental that the rates of immorality in our society apparently parallel the amount portrayed in the media? President Benson has told us that the phrase "The lusts of your eyes" in Alma 39:9 in our day means "movies, television programs, and video recordings that are both suggestive and lewd."[5] Many of the programs filling the airwaves today are both suggestive and lewd. We may well ask ourselves if lust is being instilled in our children in their own living rooms and with parental approval.

3. *Word of Wisdom Violations.* In the research on television programming, excessive use of alcohol, tobacco, and drugs was noted in 90 percent of the combined prime-time programs. Most of the usage occurred among the leading characters of the programs and among celebrities featured in commercials. What is the effect on society of these vices being portrayed as desirable and with no negative consequences?

Is the use of alcohol increasing as we see more and more advertisements and portrayals of its use? The answer is a definite yes. In 1974, 54 percent of adolescents surveyed had used alcohol; by 1982, the percent had increased to 65.2. In 1974, 81.6 percent of young adults admitted to using alcohol; in 1982, the percent was 94.6. Among adults, alcohol usage increased from 73.2 percent in 1974 to 88.2 percent in 1982.[6]

It has been estimated that 25,000 people are killed and 1.5 million are injured each year in alcohol-related automobile accidents; that 67 percent of sex crimes against children and 39 percent of sex crimes against women are alcohol-related; and that 70 percent of all drownings are alcohol-related. Some $43 billion a year is lost in medical costs, property damage, lost wages, legal fees, and other related expenses. This does not include the toll of such problems as divorce, suicide, and shattered self-image that this increasingly growing evil produces. Alcohol is the number one drug problem in America.

Why would television programs glamorize the use of alcohol and make it look so sophisticated and accepted when the harm from using it is well-documented? Though we don't know the answer to this question, we can—and must—ask ourselves, should we invite anyone into our living room who will try to entice our children to drink alcoholic beverages?

4. *Poor Academic Performance.* The amount of television children watch has also been linked to lower scores on the Scholastic Aptitude Test. Verbal scores in the last decade have dropped from 455 to 424, and math scores, from 502 to 466. Many researchers believe that TV viewing may be related to problems that children have with reading. Watching TV usually requires that the viewer do little more than stare and stay awake; it requires virtually no talent and exercises no skills that might contribute to the development of social or intellectual competence. Students who spend lots of time watching television may become accustomed to having information "spoon fed" to them instead of actively trying to obtain it through research and study. Some educators report that children who watch excessive amounts of television develop a low tolerance for learning; rather, they become accustomed to being entertained. In our own homes, could our children have better grades in school if a portion of the time spent with TV was spent doing homework or reading?

5. *Communication.* In many American homes, the first thing families do after waking in the morning is turn on the TV. The set then stays on through breakfast until children leave for school. When they return in the afternoon, the TV set is turned on again, and it is usually not turned off until bedtime. There is little opportunity for verbal interchange among family members, little opportunity for pondering important matters, sharing time and thoughts with others, or even for telling bedtime stories. The primary danger of television may lie in

the behavior it prevents rather than the behavior it produces. Turning on the TV may turn off the process that helps mold children into rational, thinking people. Many researchers are concerned that communication skills are not being allowed to develop properly. And because of lack of communication, families grow further apart.

6. *Desensitization.* A number of theories have been advanced to explain why so many people will not come to the aid of someone in distress. The results of several studies indicate that those who watch TV excessively may become, to some degree, desensitized to violence, and the natural feelings of compassion and concern are blunted. Psychiatrist Fredric Wertham has said:

> The desensitization manifests itself on different levels. Children have an inborn capacity for sympathy. But that sympathy has to be cultivated. This is one of the most delicate points in the education process. And it is this point that the mass media trample on. Even before the natural feelings of compassion have a chance to develop, the fascination of overpowering and hurting others is displayed in endless profusion. Before the soil is prepared for sympathy, the seeds of sadism are planted. The clinical result is that feelings for others are interfered with. These youngsters show a coarsening of responses and an unfeeling attitude.[7]

Ultimately, this may be one of the greatest dangers of television. Jesus taught that loving our neighbor is the second great commandment. How frightening to think that something as critical to our salvation as is this commandment could be interfered with because of repeated exposure to violence through television!

7. *Poor Nutrition.* TV commercials promote many foods that are unhealthful, such as soft drinks, potato chips and other snacks, alcoholic beverages, ice cream, and fast foods. Viewers who heed these enticing messages can develop health problems, even malnutrition. Studies by the American Dental Association indicate that 70 percent of the TV advertising aimed at children is for highly sugared snacks, candies, and breakfast

foods, while only 2 percent of the commercials promote foods essential for a balanced diet, such as milk, meat, fruits, and vegetables. In our research on prime-time programs, we found that TV characters rarely ate balanced meals; their diets usually consisted of foods and snacks low in nutritional value and high in calories. These patterns are associated with problems in weight control and nutritional deficiencies, yet the television characters eating are usually extremely thin and healthy. As Latter-day Saints, we have the great blessing of a code of health, the Word of Wisdom. The Lord wants us to take care of our bodies and eat proper foods. Have our families' eating habits been influenced or interfered with because of television?

8. *Time Consumption.* Only work and sleep rank ahead of television as a consumer of time. Recent polls indicate that the average American watches 28 hours of TV per week—a total of 1,456 hours of TV per year! With approximately 235 million people living in America, the total adds up to about 6.58 billion hours per week and 339.76 billion hours per year. What would happen if everyone in America cut his viewing time in half and spent that time in personal, family, and community involvement? Think of it: 169.8 billion hours that Americans could use to read good literature, visit friends and relatives, take classes, do volunteer work, participate in civic and church affairs, develop talents, plant gardens, and accomplish innumerable other worthwhile endeavors to build individuals, families, and society. What would our society be like if we all took the challenge to watch less TV and use the time in worthwhile causes, such as reading the scriptures daily, attending the temple regularly, becoming involved in our schools and communities, beautifying our homes, working toward a college degree, doing genealogy, learning to play a musical instrument, visiting the sick and homebound regularly, and spending more time with our families.

A recent study by the University of Michigan found that parents spend very small amounts of time reading, conversing, or playing with their children. Working mothers spend an average of 11 minutes on weekdays and 30 minutes a day on weekends; fulltime homemakers spend about 30 minutes a day on weekdays and 36 minutes a day on weekends; and fathers spend an average of 8 minutes a day on weekdays and 14 minutes a day on weekends. Maybe we need to ask ourselves if we really have time for much TV!

As Latter-day Saints we have a further warning: "Wo unto him that has the law given, yea, that has all the commandments of God, like unto us, and that transgresseth them, and that wasteth the days of his probation, for awful is his state!" (2 Nephi 9:27.)

9. *Shortened Attention Span.* In 1985 Parade Magazine surveyed elementary and secondary schoolteachers in the United States to determine their attitudes toward their careers. Teachers with at least ten years of classroom experience reported that their students today seemed to be less interested in learning and harder to teach than in the past and did not appreciate the job teachers were doing. They overwhelmingly commented that students today expected to be entertained in the classroom, had shorter attention spans, and were more responsive to visual methods of teaching.[8]

Are these teachers accurate in their assessments? Do children today really have shorter attention spans than in the past? *U.S. News and World Report* commented on this subject in an article about the effect of television: "Another difficulty is the rapid linear movement of TV images, which gives viewers little chance to pause and reflect on what they have seen. Scientists say this torrent of images also has a numbing effect, as measured electronically by the high proportion of alpha brain waves, normally associated with daydreaming or falling asleep. The result is shortened attention spans—a phenomenon increasingly lamented by teachers trying to hold the interest of students accustomed to TV."[9]

10. *Impatience.* Heavy television viewing has also been linked to impatience in viewers, by distorting the time element involved in real life. TV teaches that problems can be solved very quickly. It takes only fifteen to thirty seconds to resolve a problem on a commercial, and thirty minutes on a situation

comedy show. Many problems can be faced and solved during the course of a sixty-minute program. We get used to everything occurring in a very short time span. Researchers tell us that because of this, we become frustrated and depressed with the challenges of real life.

Many things of value take long periods of time to develop. Learning to play the piano takes years of practice. Becoming proficient at a skill or gaining a sound knowledge of the gospel takes time and patience. Our families need to develop more patience and certainly not less.

11. *Unrealistic Career Expectations.* U.S. *News and World Report* noted that "researchers have found unrealistic career expectations among people who watch a lot of TV. According to 'Television and Behavior, the new federal report': 'Heavy viewers want high status jobs, but do not intend to spend many years in school.' "[10] It may be more difficult in the future to convince young people that they need to take school seriously when the highest monetary and social rewards are reserved for the occupations of media stars in which education is often unnecessary. Are our children prepared to pay the price of success?

12. *Imitating Behavior.* Over the years numerous cases have been documented of children and adults imitating the behavior and activities they have witnessed on television programs. When I was growing up I would stand on the couch with a cape on my back and try to fly like Superman. While I used only the living room furniture for my launching pad, others have been seriously injured by trying to duplicate Superman's feat from higher starting points than mine.

Have your children ever imitated a character they have seen on TV? While some imitation may be harmless — or even desirable — a growing number of the behaviors displayed on TV can be very dangerous if imitated. The evidence seems strong that television has created major changes in our culture in such areas as fashion fads, hair styles, and music, often because viewers imitate the heroes of their favorite programs. It would seem reasonable to assume that our society also imitates the attitudes and moral values of the models provided by television.

13. *Parental and Family Roles.* With increasing numbers of broken homes and unconcerned parents in America, television has become a prime source for learning parenting roles and skills. In a day when butlers, nannies, maids, divorcées, and unmarried parents are shown rearing children on TV programs, the information being imparted may be questionable at best. Children need to learn correct parenting roles from their own parents, not from butlers, nannies, or maids.

14. *Increased Desires and Debt.* Have you or any of your children ever been influenced to buy something because you saw it advertised on television? Businesses pay huge sums of money to advertise their products on television. Do you really think companies would put out this kind of money if they didn't sell more merchandise as a result? They know that people can be influenced to buy their products through such exposure. Have your children ever asked for a particular brand of cereal because of a TV ad? Have you ever bought it? TV viewers are exposed to a never-ending parade of such enticements as cars, trucks, clothes, stereos, videos, boats, restaurant food, furniture, and medicine, as well as an endless barrage of advertisements offering easy credit and low monthly terms. Unfortunately, those who can least afford to buy are often among those who can't resist the temptation.

It has been estimated that children see more than twenty thousand TV commercials each year. On a typical Saturday morning the average American child will see approximately one hundred commercials, all trying to get them to talk their parents into buying their products. And as long as we keep buying, we are going to be bombarded with advertisements, because we have proved that they work.

15. *Blending of Ages.* Television communicates the same information to everyone at the same time, regardless of age, level of education, or experience. As a result, distinctions that have always existed between children and adults may be eroding. In a quest to hold its audience, television has increasingly

exposed that audience to material that was previously considered unsuitable for family viewing. Homosexuality, incest, adultery, cohabitation, corruption, and other formerly taboo subjects are now regularly found in the story lines. Some children now know as much about some adult subjects as adults do!

16. *Distraction.* Does TV distract us from important issues? For instance, do hostage situations deserve more air time and concern than the 1.5 million abortions performed last year? Subjects featured on the evening news frequently become the topic of conversation the next day, whether the information is important or not. We are constantly being distracted from what is really important in life. Each of us needs more time to ponder.

17. *Fear.* Do violent or horror shows produce nightmares or other fears in viewers? There is some evidence that people experience fear because of what they see on television. Reports of unrealistic fear of crime and violence have increased in recent years. What we choose to view on TV may well be the source of many of those fears.

18. *Addiction.* One educator has called television "the plug-in drug." Some professionals are now counseling and even treating patients for "media addiction." Is television as addicting as some have suggested? Can you actually become hooked on television viewing? If your family had to do without TV for an extended period of time, would there be any withdrawal pains?

19. *Physical Fitness.* The physical fitness levels of Americans, particularly young people, have been deteriorating steadily over recent years. There seems to be a definite correlation between the increased levels of television viewing and the decreased levels of physical exercise in our society. Excessive TV viewing may indeed be physically dangerous to our family's health. Do our children play as many physical games as we did when we were growing up? What muscles are being used?

CONTROLLING OUR TV VIEWING

With all the research available on the dangers and negative influence of television, we could react by eliminating it altogether in our homes. This would be a mistake. We should remember that the physical instrument—the television set—is not the cause of our problems. As newsman Edward R. Murrow once said, "A communications system is totally neutral. It has no conscience, no principle, no morality. It has only a history. It will broadcast filth or inspiration with equal facility. It will speak truth as loudly as it will speak falsehood. It is, in sum, no more or less than the men and women who use it."[11]

Television does have enormous influence, but we should not condemn the system because of the message. Those who developed the technology were undoubtedly inspired in their work. But if religious people do not use the media effectively and properly, then the antireligious will, and they will form the value systems of our country. We have the most exciting communications systems ever; the challenge is to create the messages to be used with it. Many good people work in the television industry producing shows that are inspirational and uplifting. Others are more concerned with ratings and profit than with values and principles. Television provides both types of programs—some beneficial and worthwhile and some that is of poor and even degrading quality. A problem occurs when we assume something worth watching will always be available when we turn on our TV sets. Too many people watch TV out of habit no matter what is on, and even switch stations until they find the least offending program, instead of turning the set off. When we have the TV set on, we are casting a vote that tells the television industry, through the ratings, that this is the type of program we want to see. If ratings are low for any show, you can be sure that it will not continue to be shown, because businesses will not advertise on programs no one watches.

With so many different types of programs available on TV, how can we protect our families and still enjoy the worthwhile productions? Self-discipline is essential if we are to use television for the benefit of our families.

What can be done to break the TV habit? One suggestion is to have a family council to discuss the family's involvement with TV. This might be a good time to take the following tests and discuss the findings.

TV TEST

1. Name the four children who star on the Cosby show.
2. Give me a light, a _____ _____.(Fill in blanks.)
3. Plop, plop, fizz, fizz, oh what a _____ _____ _____! (Fill in blanks.)
4. It's a good time for the great taste of _____. (Fill in blank.)
5. Who is the host of the Tonight Show?
6. Who plays a vice officer in a show set in Miami?
7. What is the name of your local TV evening news anchor?
8. Who plays the leading role on a show based in Dallas?
9. What is a Smurf?
10. Did you average 30 minutes of TV a day for the past week? (Answer yes or no).

Score 10 points for each question answered correctly or in the affirmative. Score: _____.

BOOK OF MORMON TEST

1. What are the names of the four sons of King Mosiah?
2. Alma and _____ were missionary companions in Ammonihah. (Fill in blank.)
3. _____ was the first chief judge of the Nephites. (Fill in blank.)
4. Ammon defended the flocks of King _____. (Fill in blank.)
5. Who was the last writer in the small plates of Nephi?
6. What is an onti?
7. What happened to Zeezrom after he contended with Alma?
8. Who was Nephihah?
9. Mormon gave the plates to Moroni. Who gave the plates to Mormon?
10. Do you spend 30 minutes a day reading the Book of Mormon? (Answer yes or no.)

Score 10 points for each question answered correctly or in the affirmative. (Use the index in the triple combination for references to help you answer the questions.) Score:_____.

On which test did each member of your family score the

highest? Do the members of your family know more about the scriptures or television? Some may claim it is not important to their salvation to know answers to trivia questions from the Book of Mormon. That may be true, assuming that we study the scriptures every day as our prophets have counseled us to do. And even though the trivia may not save us, a related question may be asked: Why don't we know the trivia? If we spend enough time with something, we learn both the important and the trivial points about it. If you scored higher on the TV test, how did you do it? In both cases the key is exposure. The more we are exposed to something, the more familiar we are with it. If you scored higher on the TV test, is it an indication that you watch TV more than you study the scriptures? Are the scriptures given as much emphasis and time in your home as is television? The following questions may be helpful:

1. Where is your TV located in your home? Is it the center of your most-used room?

2. Can your family live without TV and not complain about it for a day? a week? a month? a year?

3. Do you ever watch TV while eating breakfast, lunch, or dinner? How often?

4. Do you insist on silence in the room when your TV is on?

5. Does your TV ever tell you what to eat, where to go, and what to do? Do you ever follow the instructions?

6. Is your TV on when friends, home teachers, or visiting teachers come to visit, or during family prayers?

7. Have you ever stayed home from a church, school, civic, or family activity in order to watch TV?

8. Does your TV get more of your undivided attention than your children do? More than genealogy? scripture study? church assignments? community service?

9. Do the things taught on your TV reinforce the messages that the Savior taught? The messages of the General Authorities? your Sunday School class? your own parents?

10. Do you believe that your TV is helping or hindering you in your goal of reaching the celestial kingdom?

If television has become a problem in your home, what can you do about it? If you are still not sure, the following test will quickly let you know where your family stands: Unplug your TV set and put it away for seven days. That's it—end of test! If your family is addicted, you will see evidences of withdrawal symptoms, similar to those experienced by people who are addicted to tobacco, alcohol, or drugs. There will be a craving to turn the set back on. Those who are addicted won't know what to do with their spare time, and they may become restless or irritable. This is a simple, yet revealing and accurate, test. However, I have discovered that few people will take the challenge. Most will claim they don't have a problem. Others will admit they enjoy TV too much and have no desire to alter their viewing habits.

Several years ago I gave that challenge to a church group. A mother told me after the meeting that when I made the suggestion, her six-year-old son had turned to her and asked, "Mama, are we going to turn off our TV for seven days like he said?" She replied, "Yes, son, we are." He then looked at her and said, "I hate him!" Another sister called me later and said, "We have total rebellion in our neighborhood." Her family and two of her neighbors were taking the test and their children were very upset about it. But I still think it is a good test. Try it in your own home. I guarantee you will be surprised at the results.

After you have taken this seven-day test, the next step in gaining control of the TV is to view everything you watch with a pencil and paper in hand and play the "What Am I Being Taught" game. In other words, for the next seven days view every program as if you were in a school class and were preparing for a test on what you had viewed. Look for both the positive and the negative aspects of each program: record both what you see that you like and what you see that offends you.

I am convinced that once you have completed this exercise you will be ready for some family rules concerning your TV. Discuss and adopt the rules in a family council so that everyone in the family will have input. Following are some suggestions

LEARNING TO CONTROL TELEVISION 67

for rules others have used to get control of their television viewing.

SUGGESTED TV-VIEWING RULES

1. Have a purpose when you watch television. Know what you want to see before you turn the set on. Avoid "channel jumping" just to see what is on.

2. Use a TV program guide to help you determine which programs you will select. During family council, schedule in advance programs that the family can watch. Refuse to watch anything that is not scheduled.

3. Set limits on the number of hours the TV will be on in your home. Set daily and weekly viewing maximums for each individual. This will help your family be more selective in their viewing.

4. Discuss the positive and negative points of programs that are suggested for viewing. Teach children to be discriminating in their program choices.

5. Watch only programs that meet gospel standards. And remember, if a program does not meet gospel standards for children, it is not appropriate for parents either. Lead by example.

6. Never use the television as a babysitter or merely to keep yourself or children occupied.

7. Watch television *with* your children. Bring to their attention characters who solve problems by respecting others' rights and who do kind acts that could be emulated. Discuss also television characters who perform thoughtless, violent, or immoral acts. After each program, discuss what you have viewed.

8. Never watch TV during a meal. Television should not be allowed to interfere with this important time for family communication.

9. Be sure that any programs watched on Sunday are in keeping with the spirit of the Sabbath. This should apply to Monday night also.

10. Never watch anything on television that you would be

ashamed to view in person. If you would be ashamed for your children to view any scene live, you should not allow them to view it in your living room on TV.

In deciding how much TV to watch and what programs to view, ask the following questions. Sometimes a final evaluation cannot be made until after the program begins, but don't be afraid to turn the set off if the following criteria are not met.

1. Does the program encourage worthwhile ideas, values, and beliefs? Does it uphold acceptable standards of behavior and promote moral and spiritual values and respect for law, decency, and service?

2. Does the program stimulate constructive activities? Does it encourage you to learn more, to do something constructive, to be creative, to solve problems, or to work and live with others in peace and harmony?

3. Finally—and perhaps most important—is watching this particular program the best use of your time?

IDEAS FOR MAKING TV BENEFICIAL

Here are some ideas for discussion and activities based on what is seen on TV:

1. Post a world map near your television set. Point out to your children where the events are actually happening when world news is given. Discuss the situation and ask questions of your children.

2. Try to remember the names of people you see in a TV program. Quiz each other during or at the end of the program. This will be good practice for helping you remember the names of people you meet in real life.

3. Ask younger children what is happening in a program. Verbal tools can be enhanced as children describe to older family members what they think is really happening.

4. Discuss the meanings of words that are unfamiliar. Ask each other during the program the meanings of words as they come up. Have a dictionary nearby to verify the definitions.

5. Learn to discriminate between the real and unreal by discussing the situations shown in various types of programs.

6. Discuss how movie makers produce the effects seen on TV. Discuss the use of stunt men, stage make-up, and artificial means to produce desired effects.

7. Discuss how a program or behavior makes you feel. This can open a whole world of communication between parents and children. It also serves as a barometer of how their children perceive the programs they watch and the effects the programs have on them. For instance, if violence does not upset them, there is a chance they have become desensitized to it.

8. Discuss what is the intent behind a program? This may result in a more interesting exchange than the program itself, and can help families build defenses against the manipulative techniques of producers and advertisers.

9. Discuss the consequences resulting from controversial subjects that portray a decadent moral system, so that children can grow in the power of discernment between good and evil. Point out the consequences of the behaviors shown if one were to follow such a course in real life.

10. As a family, write to the sponsors of programs you view. If a program has content with questionable moral standards or ethics, let the sponsor know of your objections. Also write thank-you letters to sponsors of worthwhile programming.

11. Spend an evening listing possible activities that could be accomplished by each member of the family if the average time per person spent in watching TV (28 hours per week) were devoted to other areas. After making your list, plan which activities you will carry out.

12. Ask your children to list all the foods they see advertised on children's television. Then list all the foods they think they need to eat to be healthy. Compare the two lists and discuss the results.

IDEAS FOR CONTROLLING TV VIEWING

Here are some suggestions of things your family might do to control television watching:

1. Charge a fee for each hour of TV viewing. The greater the past abuse has been, the higher the cost will be. A bank could be placed on the TV set for this purpose. Do not use the money collected to benefit individual family members.

2. Set up a schedule for trading time. For every hour of reading (excluding homework), a child is allowed one-half hour of television. Many variations of this concept could be used, including bartering with homework, chores, and practicing an instrument.

3. Keep a small portable TV in the game closet and bring it out just as a game would be. The TV should be considered one of many entertainments that the family could choose.

4. Establish a token system, with each token worth one-half hour of television per week. Determine how many tokens each child will be allowed for the week. This will teach the children to be careful about how the tokens are used and to be selective in their viewing.

By controlling the television viewing in our homes, we can have the best of two worlds. We will have more time for communication, work, church, community service, and pleasure, yet we will be able to see the programs that will provide quality entertainment or give us valuable information.

NOTES

1. Address at the Tidewater Assembly on Family Life, Norfolk, Virginia, September 24, 1975.
2. "Worst Ad (for all of us)," *Parade*, January 5, 1986, p. 6.
3. *Statistical Abstract of the United States, 1986* (Washington: U.S. Bureau of the Census, 1985).
4. *Statistical Abstract of the United States*, 1976, 1986.
5. *Ensign*, May 1986, p. 45.
6. *Statistical Abstract of the United States*, 1986.
7. *Where Do You Draw the Line?*, Victor B. Cline, ed., (Provo: Brigham Young University Press, 1974), p. 165.
8. Marguerite Michaels, "Report Card from Our Teachers," *Parade*, December 1, 1985, p. 5.

9. "What Is TV Doing to America?", *U.S. News and World Report*, August 2, 1982, p. 28.
10. Ibid.
11. Frank J. Kohn, ed., *Documents of American Broadcasting*, 3rd ed. (Englewood Cliffs, New Jersey: Prentice Hall, 1978), pp. 251-61.

CHAPTER 6

RATING THE MOVIES

Some time ago, in preparation for a presentation to seminary students on the influence of movies, I decided to attend one of the movies that were currently popular with teenagers. In selecting the movie, I looked for one that had an acceptable rating from the rating board of the Motion Picture Association of America and that was recommended by some young Latter-day Saints. When I talked to them, it soon became obvious what my choice should be. The movie I selected was not only their favorite but was popular with many older Saints as well. One college student told me she had been to it five times and wanted to see it again.

In selecting this movie, I felt fairly safe, since it met my rating criterion as well as had high recommendation from friends. But as a further precaution, I asked the student who had seen it five times some specific questions. What about profanity? "That was the thing that I really liked about it," she said. "It had only one four-letter word in the entire movie." And illicit sex scenes? There were none, she told me. Though I now had it straight from one of my students that the movie would be acceptable, I decided to take one last precaution. I put a pencil and notebook in my pocket before I went to the movie.

When the film started I found that the music and the sound effects were far superior to anything I had previously heard at a theater, and the scenery was beautiful. But I'll admit that I didn't see every detail of the movie. I was so busy keeping track of the offensive material in my notebook that I spent a large portion of my time looking down. The male lead was a handsome young man, one who might be a role model for boys and very attractive to girls. But there were serious problems with the character he portrayed. The character drank heavily, was immoral, and did whatever was necessary to get to the top of his profession. And what about my student's recommendation and her claim that she heard only one four-letter word and saw no scenes depicting sex? I'll admit she did have one of the numbers right in the profanity count—the movie did include one. In fact, I found that there were actually ninety-one profane words, including thirty-three that took the Lord's name in vain. And one bedroom scene was so graphic that I still can't believe the movie was rated PG (parental guidance).

How could anyone sit and watch a movie like this and not notice the offensive language or the immoral scene? I don't claim to know all the answers, but I do believe that the word *exposure* is a key. When we are constantly exposed to something, we can become calloused to it. This certainly applies to things that are offensive; eventually we may even begin to call evil good, and fail to recognize such things as unnatural. Some researchers call this *desensitization*. But by whatever name we call it, the fact remains that repeated exposure will result in this condition. An analogy might be made with a man who labors heavily all day and gets callouses on his hands: the person who is constantly exposed to movies with questionable content can similarly develop a calloused mind. The abhorrence and pain associated with the material soon leave, making it extremely difficult to recognize right from wrong.

At Brigham Young University's Education Week, I told the following experience, which illustrates this point. A few years ago a man whom I really admire called and asked if my two sons and I wanted to go to a movie with him and his sons. He and his wife had seen the movie three days earlier, and he assured me it had nothing offensive except two or three profanities. Finally I agreed to go. I did, however, take my little notebook, in case I needed to keep count. Several times during the movie I looked over at my sons, and they looked back at me sheepishly. You see, this good father had missed a little on his count of profanity. Instead of two or three words, there were forty-six.

In my talk at Education Week, I asked how this fine, active Latter-day Saint could have missed such filthy language when it was so apparent. After my talk, many people wrote and shared their own observations. One man wrote: "That evening several young people from our ward who were attending Education Week with us went off campus and rented a video recorder and a movie to watch in the lounge of our dorm. We parents were in the same lounge, discussing the classes we had attended; and having just come from your class, I was keenly aware of the amount of profane language in the movie the kids were watching. I was even more shocked to see that everyone else in the room seemed totally oblivious toward it."

After receiving this letter, I rented the movie myself, having first determined that it had received a rating that indicated it was suitable for anyone over age thirteen. The plot, I discovered, revolved around an immoral premise from start to finish, with considerable obscene language. Almost everything we are taught in the gospel was mocked and ridiculed in the film. Needless to say, I still wonder how any group of Latter-day Saint parents could sit in a room where this movie was playing and be oblivious to its content.

A woman from Utah wrote: "I went to see a movie while at Education Week and decided to take notes. Here are my results: references to illicit sex, 15; swearing or vulgar language, 23; consumption of alcoholic beverages, 6; stealing, 1; extreme violence, 1. I never really did understand the message of the movie. The sad truth is that if I hadn't heard your lecture, I probably would have watched it and enjoyed it. Thank you for helping me by making me aware of what the media are doing to us."

And another woman wrote: "I was in a video shop last year and heard three clean-cut young men talking to each other in the adult-movie section. Two of them told the third young man, 'Oh, you won't enjoy that movie until you have been home from your mission at least a year.' "

Alexander Pope stated: "Vice is a monster of so frightful mien, / As to be hated needs but to be seen; / Yet seen too often, familiar with her face, / We first endure, then pity, then embrace." It is obvious to me that some people have gone way past the endurance stage by repeated exposure to inappropriate films. How can some not see the immorality and not hear the obscenities? In addition to the problem of desensitization, many have another problem: rationalization. Sometimes even after we have been made aware of a problem, we rationalize our way out of it by saying, "It's not that big a deal" or "Everyone else is doing it too."

I once overheard two young women discussing a highly controversial R-rated movie. One of them mentioned that she had seen it with her mother. Her friend exclaimed, "You mean to tell me you saw that movie with your mother?" "Yes, I did," was the reply. The friend then sheepishly admitted that she too had seen the movie—but, she added, "I sure wouldn't see it with my mother." Isn't it sad that this young woman wouldn't consider attending a movie with her mother that she herself had seen.

Occasionally I hear other young people rationalize their attendance at undesirable movies. Some argue that the movies just reflect what is happening in society. Others ask, "Aren't we supposed to be well informed and see what's happening in the world around us? We can't live in a shell." Probably the most common rationalization is used in reference to profanity. I have heard many young people and even adults use this one:

"We hear this type of language every day of the week at school and at work. What's so wrong with hearing it in a movie?" Is this a good point or is it a rationalization? When I hear young people make such comments, I sometimes use the following illustration:

"Suppose you walked out that front door and saw a streaker running by. You didn't mean to see her, and you immediately turned away and prayed for help to get the incident out of your mind. Do you think Heavenly Father would hold you accountable for that, knowing you didn't mean to see her and you were trying to get it out of your mind? Why?

"Now suppose you walked out that front door and saw a streaker running by. But instead of turning away, you stared and watched her every move, finding it hard to believe she was actually doing this. After a few minutes, with your eyes straining to get a last look, she finally faded from sight. You then made no effort to get the incident out of your mind, and even told your friends about it. Do you think Heavenly Father will hold you accountable for this incident, knowing that you didn't really mean to see her when you first opened the door? Why?

"Finally, imagine you read in the local newspaper and heard from several of your friends that at a particular time today a streaker was going to run through the downtown area. Do you think Heavenly Father would or would not hold you accountable if you paid a $4.50 admission fee to see her? Why?"

Satan is cunning. He can make rationalizations seem so logical, when in reality they are covering up for something totally wrong. It is true that evil things are happening in our society. It is also true that many of us are forced to listen to obscene language in the schools and workplace. But we will each be judged by the intent of our heart. In likening this illustration to movies, I do not believe the Lord will hold us accountable for seeing or hearing something inappropriate in a movie that we did not intend to see, if we will get up and walk away and pray for help in getting it out of our minds. Consider, however, what might be our reaction if we didn't realize that there would be objectionable scenes, but when they did appear, we made no effort to leave or to get them out of our minds. Is this the same as or different from walking away from the film? And finally, there should be no question about the intent for those who know that the immoral scenes are in the movie and still choose to see them. By the intent of their hearts, they have chosen to view material that has been condemned by living prophets and the scriptures.

The question now arises: who is responsible for the material shown in many of our modern movies? Are the movie producers to blame? Are the performers to blame? Not entirely. Theater goers ultimately decide which films will be produced, because they ultimately pay all the bills. We need to ask ourselves what we are paying the actors and actresses to do on the screen. When we attend degrading movies, aren't we essentially saying that we will pay the price of admission if they will act immorally or violently or talk in a vulgar manner for us? Even more troubling questions may be asked in light of research that suggests that movies and TV programs to some extent teach values and actions that are modeled or imitated in our society. If this is true, then the implications could be frightening.

For instance, if we pay an admission fee to show our support for a film that includes illicit sex and then someone in the audience becomes immoral because of the emotions produced in that dark theater, are we actually accessories to the sin, since we helped pay the bill to produce the film through our admission fee? What about violence and crime?

We should be careful how we cast our votes and try to remember how powerful movies can be for good or for evil. One of the most dramatic examples of this power came from the movie *E.T.* The movie's producers went to a major candy manufacturer to try to get a promotional tie-in between one of that company's products and the hero of a new science-fiction movie. The offer was turned down. The producers then approached another candy manufacturer, which accepted the offer and paid no money for the movie plug. Two weeks after the film was released, sales of the candy featured in the film increased dramatically.

I asked the students of a seminary class what kind of candy E.T. had eaten in the movie. They all replied almost in unison with the answer. One boy told me, "After I had seen that movie, I ate that candy every day for a month." I asked him how many times he had eaten that brand of candy before he saw the movie. He replied, "I had never even heard of it before the movie."

This example illustrates just how powerful movies can be. If movies can sell candy, can they also sell immorality? What if the hero smokes marijuana? On the other hand, surely movies can also be used to teach great moral values and lift us to new heights of love, kindness, and other desirable traits.

To me, one of the greatest inventions to help us in using movies to benefit our families is the videocassette recorder (VCR). My family has been greatly blessed by some of the classic musicals, the adventure films, and the inspirational films we have seen. We can watch stories from Church history, the Bible, the Book of Mormon, and the other Church-produced movies right in our own home. We have now visited Israel, various Church history spots, the Polynesian Cultural Center—all without ever leaving our own living room. I have no doubt that the Lord inspired the inventors of this and other tools of the media. But we must realize that the adversary is also aware of how influential these tools are.

At a local Education Day program, I mentioned the benefits in owning a VCR if we take advantage of the good movies and programs that are now available. After the program, three women came up to talk to me. They agreed that VCRs are a benefit, but only if they are controlled and used wisely. I had, of course, realized this before the program, but had failed to point it out in my talk. Then one of the women made a good observation. She said, "You know, there are only so many good movies available at most video rental stores. I found that after our family had viewed all the movies in the family section, we began to let some that were not so family oriented into our home." She continued, "I see now that we are allowing movies to be shown in our home that we would never have dreamed of allowing a few years ago." The other women agreed that the same thing had happened in their homes. One added, "Until today I hadn't realized what was happening, because it has been so gradual that I didn't even notice it."

We must always be aware that our families can be greatly affected by the things to which we choose to expose ourselves. Imagine, if you will, that you have teenagers in your home. One day they come home and ask if they can go to a party at the home of a popular kid at school. You have never heard of the boy who is giving the party. Would you let your teenager attend with no further questions asked, or would you want to know more about the party? Now, suppose you learned that at many such parties there is drinking, profanity, smoking, drug use, immorality, nudity, and even some violence. Our prophet has also warned that to be exposed to such vices will affect one's spirituality. Now, would you let your children go to the party after hearing these warnings? What if they promised they wouldn't do anything wrong and that they would remember who they were—would you then let them go? Obviously most parents would not let our children attend this type of party no matter how many times they asked or even pleaded. But isn't this similar to what is happening with certain movies? The party is in our hometowns, but it's at a movie theater. The popular kids throwing it are called movie producers and movie stars. Should we allow our children to attend these parties without even checking into them?

Dr. Victor L. Cline, a professor of psychology at the University of Utah, concluded after years of research on this subject, "I am personally convinced by a vast amount of research that the images, fantasies and models which we are repeatedly exposed to in our advertisements, our entertainments, our novels, our motion pictures, and other works of art can and do powerfully affect the self-image, and later the behavior, of nearly all young people and adults too."[1] If movies can affect self-image and behavior, it seems critical to our families' survival that we recognize this fact and take the steps necessary to make this powerful influence a positive instead of a negative one.

HOW MOVIES ARE RATED

Some of my most pleasant memories of youth revolved around good movies. I can still remember some of the films I saw and the joy they brought into my life. There was no bad language, no nudity, and, for the most part, good always triumphed in the end. But even then, I now realize, we were being conditioned to accept things that were inappropriate. Movies have almost always depicted violence as a natural part of life, with many westerns, war, and crime themes. Over the years moviegoers were exposed to increasing violence until many went from abhorrence to endurance. Most of us justified our viewing of these scenes because we thought that was how life really was. We were being conditioned to believe that murders, beatings, and other violence and crime made a movie acceptable so long as there were no scenes depicting sex.

In the early 1960s, with the growth of television eating away at audiences and profits, the movie industry faced a dilemma. How could movies attract audiences when people could stay at home and watch films on TV? With society conditioned to violence, the movie industry tested the market with more sexually explicit material to try to keep audiences. The trend began with the foreign movie distributors but soon spread to the American film companies.

A movement was begun in the movie industry to alter the 1934 Motion Picture code, which had stated: "Pictures shall not infer that low forms of sex relationships are the accepted or common thing." The code was revised, and soon movies featuring top stars were being made on abortion, prostitution, drug addiction, extramarital affairs, and many other subjects that had previously been taboo. It wasn't until 1967 that a highly respected actress let a four-letter profanity slip out of her mouth. Soon floodgates were opened, and tremendous pressure came from within the industry to abandon totally the old movie code.

On November 1, 1968, the Motion Picture Association of America gave in to the pressure, and a new voluntary classification was adopted. Each film from that point on would be viewed by a seven-member board and given a rating of G (for general audiences), PG (parental guidance advised), R (restricted to viewers age seventeen and over), and X (rating denied because the movie exceeded the standards of the other classifications). PG-13 (parental guidance for viewers age thirteen and over) was later added.

Although in theory this system seems to be a good idea, the flaws are readily apparent. The judges, who are the single source of the ratings, are concerned about theme, language, violence, and sex and nudity in the movies submitted. The final judgment is by majority vote, and one person's vote can make the difference in the rating a movie receives. To place total trust in the ratings of this seven-member board seems very risky for Latter-day Saint families, since the judges are not aware of—or concerned about—our Latter-day Saint values, goals, and objectives.

Another problem with the ratings system is that over the years the rating standards have eroded as society has become increasingly permissive and lax regarding moral values. This is reflected in situations in which some movies that received the X rating when the code first went into effect were subsequently released several years later with the PG rating!

Even as early as 1971-72, the deterioration was apparent. Dr. Cline and four research assistants analyzed 37 films in a survey of motion pictures playing in Salt Lake City. Of the movies, 16 percent were X-rated, 24 percent were rated R, 46 percent were rated PG, and 14 percent were rated G. The researchers found that the average film contained 38 scenes or incidents of violence and sex. In 57 percent of the films, dishonesty was presented in a "heroic light" or as "justifiable conduct in light of the hero's circumstances." In 43 percent of the films, the heroes were law breakers or antisocial characters. In 59 percent, the heroes killed one or more persons. In 60 percent, premarital and extramarital sexual relations were depicted as normal and acceptable. And 70 percent of the male leads and 72 percent of female leads were depicted as sexually promiscuous.[2] The situation has changed even more drastically in the years since this survey. For instance, I recently read the following review in a respected national magazine: "Recommended for 10 years old and up. . . . Raw language and sexual remarks, violence and a troubling scene in which a teenager dies of a heroin overdose. . . . A lovely, funny, fairy-like story."

But probably the most dangerous thing that has come out of the ratings system has been the confidence placed in it by moviegoers. Although it should be apparent that the system is unreliable, to many it is the ultimate guide to what they see or what they allow their children to see. Many justify and rationalize seeing violent, vulgar, obscene, and even pornographic movies because of so-called good ratings. If we are to protect our families, we should be extremely careful about the movies we view or allow our families to view, regardless of the ratings.

Occasionally I ask students in my classes to define pornography. So far, not one has ever given me the dictionary's definition of the word. In the *American Heritage Dictionary*, pornography is defined as "written or pictorial matter intended to arouse sexual feelings." Some people tend to believe that a movie must be rated XXX to qualify as pornographic. Is this true, according to this definition? I believe that pornography can easily exist in films that have so-called good ratings.

When our prophets speak out against pornography, are they speaking of only the triple-X variety, or do they mean "any material intended to arouse sexual feelings"? Do you think President Kimball really thought about the ratings of movies when he made the following statement: "Each person must keep himself clean and free from lusts. He must shun ugly, polluted thoughts and acts as he would an enemy. Pornography and erotic stories and pictures are worse than polluted food. Shun them. The body has power to rid itself of sickening food. That person who entertains filthy stories or pornographic pictures and literature records them in his marvelous human computer, the brain, which can't forget this filth. Once recorded, it will always remain there, subject to recall—filthy images."[3]

In recent years I have tried to persuade some of the young people I deal with that pornography has a broader meaning than we sometimes apply to it, and we need to be careful not to put pornographic images into our minds, because they will remain with us. I particularly remember trying to convince one young woman that some of the movies she was attending could be dangerous to her. I was very proud of her later when she received a mission call. Maybe the movies hadn't affected her after all, I thought. But when she arrived home after serving eighteen months, she made a most interesting comment. She said, "I sure wish I had listened to you about those movies you tried to warn me about. When I arrived in the mission field, several times as I began to teach the missionary discussions, all that would come to my mind was the filthy images in the movies I had attended before my mission. I would have to turn the discussion over to my companion because I was unable to teach." She then said she would never go to another inappropriate movie again. I hope she has kept her resolve.

We are affected greatly by the things to which we choose to expose ourselves. Dr. Cline has written:

> What starts out as a spectator sport introduces into one's brain a vast library of antisocial fantasies. These have the potential, much research suggests, of eventually being acted out—to the destruction of the individual and others around him.
>
> I have found that four things typically happen to some people who become immersed in erotic or pornographic material. First, they become addicted. They get hooked on it and come back for more and more. Second, their desire for it escalates. They soon need rougher and more explicit material to get the same kicks and excitement. Third, they become desensitized to the abnormality of the behavior portrayed. In time, they accept and embrace what at first had shocked and offended them. Fourth, eventually there is a tendency and temptation to act out what they have witnessed. Appetite has been whetted and conscience anesthetized.[4]

If we are to protect our families from the negative influence of inappropriate movies, we must become more aware of what is happening. Satan's thrust is at young people, for it is among them that he will have his greatest success. The majority of moviegoers today are teenagers and young adults. According to one author, 20 percent are 12 to 15, 29 percent are 16 to 20, and 27 percent are 21 to 29. This means that 76 percent are under 30![5] The message of these figures is obvious. Parents rarely, if ever, attend movies, and therefore their awareness level of the content is severely reduced. With parents secure at home and relying on the ratings, the movie industry has fallen to new lows in what is now produced and shown in theaters, with almost no protest from the parents.

The words of President Joseph Fielding Smith are even more true today than when he said them more than two decades ago: "Never in the history of the... church have there been so many temptations, so many pitfalls, so many dangers to lure away the members of the church from the path of duty and from righteousness, as we find today."[6] And President Ezra Taft Benson has warned: "Today because some parents have refused to become informed and then stand up and inform their children, they are witnessing the gradual physical and spiritual destruction of their posterity. If we would become like God, knowing good and evil, then we had best find out what is undermining us, how to avoid it, and what we can do about it."[7]

PROTECTING OUR FAMILIES

How can we, as parents, protect ourselves, our children, and our communities from the flood of erotic and obscene material that is found in all too many movies, television shows, and other media? First, I believe it will require some steps that some are not willing to do, but that are a critical part to any protection plan. These steps are prayer, planning, and work.

Imagine, if you will, that a salesman knocks on your door and says he is representing a local health spa. In his presentation, he convinces you that the spa includes everything you need to keep physically fit—a jogging track, racquetball court, swimming pool, weight room, and so on. Being interested in physical fitness, and especially in developing bigger muscles, you decide to join the spa. You decide you can spend two hours a day three days a week, a total of six hours. When you go to the weight room, you pull up a chair and watch others work out for two hours. How many muscles would you build by watching others work out six hours a week? If you were to increase the time to 12 hours a week, would you get the desired results? How about if you watched others work out for 20 or 36 or 50 hours? You could spend all the time you want visiting the spa and watching others work out, but the muscle development you want will come only after *you* get to work.

This analogy might be applied to the teachings of the gospel. It is fine that we go to church every week and watch the proceedings for three hours; this is a critical part of the plan. But, as in the health spa example, we shouldn't expect to develop our spiritual muscles until we actually get to work. In like manner, if we are to avoid the flood of temptations that are coming toward our families through the media, we need to pray, develop a plan of action, and then actually get to work.

Since prayer is discussed in detail in the scriptures and in the teachings of our prophets, I won't attempt to add anything here except to encourage you to make this the beginning of any plan. And work is something only you can do, after you know your plan. Let's concentrate, then, on some suggestions for a plan to assist your family in avoiding the temptations so prevalent today.

One starting point is to call the family together to discuss the threats involved with objectionable material and establish some criteria to help us make wise decisions. Meetings of this nature are more productive and beneficial if everyone in the family, including teenagers, is involved and allowed to contribute ideas and solutions in an open atmosphere. Those who help formulate family rules are more likely to abide by them.

The following are ideas that may be helpful in establishing family guidelines.

1. *Know the content.* Before you attend, buy, rent, or borrow any movie, learn all you can about its content. Many magazines and newspapers have movie reviews that may be helpful. You might also talk with people who have seen the film. Ask specific questions: What was the language like? Any violence? Any immorality? Who are the stars? What other movies have they appeared in? Call the theater and ask the staff there about the movie. By carefully selecting the movies we view, we can increase the chance that our experiences will be uplifting and wholesome. Remember, if you still have doubts after you make your inquiries, the best advice may be to not see it.

2. *Require parental permission.* Young people should have their parents' permission whenever they view any movie, whether at the theater or at a friend's home.

3. *Reject anything that is obscene.* Agree that you will get up and walk out of a movie if anything obscene is depicted. Most theaters will refund your money if you are offended by the material in a film. If the obscene material occurs on a video, agree that you will turn it off immediately.

4. *Ask, how would you feel if . . . ?* Ask before attending or during every movie you see if this is the type of movie you would feel comfortable seeing if your bishop or the prophet were sitting beside you. If you feel embarrassed, then choose another movie, one that you *would* feel good about.

5. *Ask, Will it make a difference?* Always ask will it make any difference in a few years if you see the movie or not, even if everyone else you know is attending. Too often we subject our minds to material that becomes part of our thoughts just because everyone else is doing it. Choose only those movies that will help make you a better person, regardless of what others may do.

6. *Avoid that "one bad scene."* How often have you heard someone say, "It was a great movie if it hadn't been for the one bad scene," or "It has a good message if you can get past the filthy language." Avoid such films. Remember that Satan will give you many truths just to get in his one lie. Think back on a movie you have seen with "just one bad scene." If you

can still see the scene in your mind, it has nullified any temporary pleasure you may have received from viewing it.

7. *Apply Moroni's counsel in Moroni 7:16-18:* "For behold, the Spirit of Christ is given to every man, that he may know good from evil; wherefore, I show unto you the way to judge; for everything which inviteth to do good, and to persuade to believe in Christ, is sent forth by the power and gift of Christ; wherefore ye may know with a perfect knowledge it is of God. But whatsoever thing persuadeth men to do evil, and believe not in Christ, and deny him, and serve not God, then ye may know with a perfect knowledge it is of the devil; for after this manner doth the devil work, for he persuadeth no man to do good, no, not one; neither do his angels; neither do they who subject themselves unto him."

Each member of our family needs to become a movie critic with this counsel in mind. You can have your own rating board, with your family as members of the board. Develop your own criteria for rating movies, and give each one you watch a rating of G, PG, PG-13, R, X. Based on your criteria, a movie rated PG by the seven-member MPAA board may well be rated X by your family's board!

You might want to try viewing movies and TV shows with a pencil and some paper in hand, so you can analyze the content. You will be amazed at the messages—both good and bad—you will pick out. In analyzing the content, use gospel principles to determine what is negative and what is positive. Here are some aspects to consider:

1. *Theme.* What do you believe is the purpose or the message of the movie or program? Why did the producers spend so much money to bring you this message? How would you characterize the overall message—good, bad, spiritual, silly, patriotic, or what?

2. *Language.* What kind of language is used? Are people respectful in communicating with one another? Or do they ridicule or mock? Are off-color or vulgar jokes or dialogue included? How many profane words are used? Is the Lord's name used in vain? How many times? Note: If you have never

listened closely to the language you are exposed to in the media, you may be in for a big surprise when using this idea.

3. *Violence.* How many acts of violence are there? Why were they included? Are they essential to the plot?

4. *Sex and Nudity.* Was premarital or extramarital sex shown or implied? Were there any portrayals of couples living together unmarried? How were the heroes portrayed—sexually promiscuous or virtuous? Were there any consequences for immorality? What were those consequences?

5. *Other Inappropriate Behavior.* How much drug, tobacco, and alcohol abuse is shown? How are marriage and family life portrayed? How are the heroes and heroines portrayed? What crimes were committed and what were the consequences?

I am convinced that once you and your family have established your guidelines and have watched a movie critically and using a pencil and paper to keep counts and make notes, you will never see things in the same way again. Messages that are good will be appreciated more than ever before, while those that are evil will almost jump out at you from the screen. You will see things that you have never seen before, and in the process you will build up a wall of protection as you become more aware and eliminate from your viewing those films that do not meet your standards.

NOTES

1. Address at Tidewater Assembly on Family Life, Norfolk, Virginia.

2. Victor L. Cline, "How Do Movies and TV Influence Behavior," *Ensign* October 1972, pp. 14-15.

3. Edward L. Kimball, ed., *Teachings of Spencer W. Kimball* (Salt Lake City: Bookcraft, 1982), p. 283.

4. Victor L. Cline, "Obscenity—How It Affects Us, How We Can Deal with It," *Ensign*, April 1984, p. 32.

5. David Pirie, *Anatomy of the Movies* (New York: Macmillan, 1981), p. 14.

6. Joseph Fielding Smith, *Take Heed to Yourselves* (Salt Lake City: Deseret Book, 1966), p. 127.

7. Ezra Taft Benson, *God, Family, Country* (Salt Lake City: Deseret Book, 1975), pp. 229-30.

CHAPTER 7

THE CHALLENGE OF MODERN MUSIC

In 1968 at the height of the war in Vietnam, I received a letter that read in part, "Greetings! You have been inducted into the United States Army." I have never felt sicker than I did the day I reported for active duty at Ft. Bliss, Texas. Although we went to bed that night at eleven, I found it difficult to sleep as I lay thinking of my home, family, and friends. At exactly 3:30 the next morning, all the lights in the room went on and a drill sergeant began hitting the metal railings of the bunk beds with a metal rod. I have never before nor since wanted so much to be home in my own bed as I did that first morning of basic training.

After making our beds and eating breakfast, we were marched over to a large auditorium for orientation. An officer told us how proud we should feel to be serving in the U.S. army, but I thought to myself, "I'm not proud to be in the army. I just want to be home."

Next, we watched some films on our military history and

previous war efforts. I was still convinced that I didn't want to be there, no matter how much they played on my emotions. Then a strange thing happened. The curtains on the stage opened to reveal a military band. After a short introduction, the band began to play patriotic songs. At first I still had negative feelings about the whole situation. I said to myself, "Okay, I kind of like the music they're playing, but I still hate army life. I want to go home." But the more the band played, the more I could feel my attitude changing. Soon I found myself thinking, "Maybe this place isn't so bad after all. Maybe I really should be here to do my part." By the end of the concert, when the band played "The Battle Hymn of the Republic," I thought, "You know, the army isn't so bad. I fact, I think I like it here."

After the program ended that day and we walked out into the 105-degree heat, my homesickness returned. But in that auditorium that day, I learned a valuable lesson in life. I learned that music is a very important part of our lives and can be a very powerful tool. In fact, it was so powerful that at least temporarily this music had totally altered my emotions and feelings to the point that I was not even afraid to go to war — at least as long as the music was playing.

Music has been called the universal language, because it speaks directly to our emotions. Our emotions and feelings can, in turn, actually influence our behavior.

History is replete with examples of the power of music. When Christ needed strength to face his terrible ordeal in the Garden of Gethsemane, he turned to music. The scriptures record, "And when they had sung an hymn, they went out into the mount of Olives." (Matthew 26:30.) Joseph Smith also turned to music before facing his death. One of the last things he did in Carthage Jail was to ask John Taylor to sing a song. And in our day, music plays an important role in our church services and activities.

Today, more than ever, music is involved in many aspects of our lives. It would be very unusual to go for even one day without hearing some form of music. We hear music in our homes and cars; in restaurants, department stores, elevators, and doctors' offices; on TV and radio; and at almost every public event, including sports. It has been reported that the average American listens to the radio for approximately twenty-five hours a week.

Over the years, I've observed a few things about music that to me are quite remarkable. Have you ever noticed that regardless of the message of a song, if you like the rhythm and beat, you can listen to it over and over again without tiring of it? This is not usually true with the spoken word. When we hear stories, experiences, and even jokes that we have heard before, how many times have we thought to ourselves, "Oh boy, here we go again with a story I've already heard." Often when this happens, we immediately turn the speaker off. Yet when we put music to words, something almost magical happens. Instead of being bored or annoyed at the repetition, we tend to enjoy it even more with repeated exposure. Have you ever heard teenagers call a radio station to ask that a particular song not be played again because they have already heard it? Something inherent in music can make repeated exposure to the message enjoyable. And once we have heard a song repeated many times, the words may remain with us for the rest of our lives.

In a lecture at BYU Education Week about the power of music, I asked class members to try to fill in the words to songs that had been popular many years ago. As I read the first words in the songs, almost every person in the room completed the lines. Let's try the same test here and see if you can fill in the blanks:

1. It was a one-eyed, one-horned, flying purple _____.
2. Does your chewing gum lose its flavor on the _____?
3. You ain't nothing but a _____.
4. Love me tender, love me _____.
5. Yesterday, all my troubles seemed so _____.
6. Please, Mr. Custer, I don't _____.
7. Do you know the way to _____?
8. Rock around the _____.
9. Twist and _____.
10. I left my heart in _____.

In the Education Week class, I asked one woman, who appeared to be in her late forties, when she had last heard one of the songs mentioned above. She replied that it had been while she was in high school, nearly thirty years ago, yet she remembered the words as if it were only yesterday.

When words are put to music, our ability to recall those words increases greatly. This point was demonstrated in a seminary class I once taught. One of the challenges in teaching seminary is to help the students learn and remember the forty basic scriptures for the year. For one class, I divided the scriptures up equally among the students and let them teach their assigned scriptures to the rest of the class. The students used various methods to teach their scriptures to one another, but the students who used music in their presentations were by far the most successful.

I can still see Letitia Alvis as she came to the front of the class and turned on a cassette tape of a song she had recorded the night before to the tune of "The Bear Went Over the Mountain." She started out singing her song very slowly and then got faster and faster as the song progressed. Try it!

> The stone cut out of the mountain,
> The stone cut out of the mountain,
> The stone cut out of the mountain,
> Daniel two, four four, four five.
> Daniel two, four four, four five;
> Daniel two, four four, four five.
> The stone cut out of the mountain,
> The stone cut out of the mountain,
> The stone cut out of the mountain,
> Daniel two, four four, four five.

I don't think I will ever forget the scripture or the reference: Daniel 2:44-45, "The stone cut out of the mountain."

Another student, David Packard, conducted a round for one of his assigned scriptures. He divided the class into two sides. Then one side of the class started the song, and, at the end of the first line, the other side started singing. They sang to the tune of "Three Blind Mice":

> For I am not ashamed
> Of the gospel of Christ,
> For it's salvation to all who believe,
> To the Jew first and also the Greek,
> This is the scripture to learn this
> week,
> Romans 1:16
> For I am not ashamed.

We sang this song through twice and had a little contest to determine which side of the class sang the best. I can assure you that I have not forgotten David's scripture, Romans 1:16, and the key words: "For I am not ashamed of the gospel of Christ."

But as great a tool as music is for building spirituality, lifting our spirits, and helping us learn and remember positive messages, it can also be dangerous when used in the wrong way. Music is one of the deadliest weapons the adversary has in his vast arsenal. With its power, he can create a sugar-coated poison that can slowly destroy our spirituality and that of our families. If we can remember the messages and words to songs for extended periods of time and perhaps for a lifetime, what effect will these messages then have on us if they are negative or immoral? This seems to be what has happened to much of our modern music.

Edward Jay Whetmore has commented on this problem: "Rock lyrics are learned by rote — that is, through repetition. Lyrics that may be barely recognizable the first time around usually become quite clear by the 10th, 20th or 200th time. Both AM and FM rock stations tend to play relatively few songs, most of them by just a handful of superstars. That way we hear the same songs over and over again, and we can't help learning the words. Millions of Americans share the same words and ideas simultaneously."[1]

Illicit sex, divorce, drugs and alcohol abuse are common topics of many popular songs. But we make a mistake when we say that the problem lies only in a certain type of music. Immoral messages can be found in many types of music, and we would do well not to point the finger at just the music of teenagers. When questionable lyrics are pointed out, the standard answer for many people is, "Yes, I know the words are bad, but I don't listen to the words. I just like the music and the beat." According to research in this area, this simply is not true. Our brains are very perceptive, and we actually pick up the messages, whether we are conscious of it or not. It seems improbable that we could listen to a song repeatedly without recording the message in our minds.

Recent surveys have indicated that over 70 percent of all popular songs are about what the world would call love. But on a closer examination, we find that many are not actually about love at all, but about lust. I recently purchased a magazine containing the lyrics to eighty-one popular songs of our day. In analyzing the messages, I found that forty-one of the songs had messages about either premarital or extramarital sex. But that's not all. Some of the songs also included messages about violence, drugs, drinking, smoking, homosexuality, incest, and rape.

If there are any doubts about the influence of some of the current popular music, I think we can judge it by its fruits. The perversions of its practitioners are well documented and should be enough to condemn its powerful influence. But even with these obvious signs of danger, some young people still fall into its dangerous traps. Recently a controversial hard-rock group appeared in concert in our area. I was hoping that no Latter-day Saints would attend, though I knew, as I visited the seminary classes in our area, that the concert was generating excitement. After the concert I learned that several LDS teenagers had attended with complete approval of their parents. I asked one of the teenagers to write a brief description of the concert. This is his response:

> The concert was one of the best concerts I have ever attended. I might even venture to say that it was the best! The light show was superb! They had green lasers that created excellent special effects. I thought the concert, as a whole, was great. The rest of the crowd apparently thought

it was good also, because they were screaming and yelling and applauding for more. There were a few distractions like the haze of marijuana smoke and the girls who threw underwear and bras and class rings up onto the stage. But even with these minor distractions, I thought the concert was well worth the money I spent on it. The tickets were $16 apiece and I took an LDS girl as my date. We also bought T shirts for $14 each. Counting gas, I spent around $65.

This evaluation was written by a boy whose father is out of work, but who still went with parental permission. Music indeed has a drawing power among youth. I wonder if we realize the dangerous effects that attending this type of concert can have on them. I challenge every parent to become more aware of the music that we and members of our families listen to. We can help our families stay strong if we are aware of music's power, use it as a positive tool, and screen out the negative aspects. We must be willing to take the time to find out what type of music our children are buying or listening to. Record producers are in the business for profit, and if enough people refuse to buy inappropriate records, profits will drop and changes will definitely come. But as long as undesirable records continue to sell, there will be a problem. And as long as people will pay to attend objectionable concerts, the groups that perform them will continue.

Over the past several years I've had the opportunity to talk to many youth groups about music, its influences, and why we must be careful in its use. Here are a few ideas I've found effective in demonstrating this point.

Music can drive the Spirit out or bring the Spirit in. I demonstrated this to a group that had just returned from a spiritual temple trip. I told them to take two or three minutes to think of the most spiritual part of the trip. As soon as I gave this assignment, I turned on a cassette tape and played a popular song at a fairly high volume. As soon as the song ended, I called on the stake president's son to describe his spiritual experience. He said, "I don't have one to relate. No matter how hard I tried, I couldn't think of anything spiritual while that music was playing." I pointed out that some music does drive the Spirit away.

Later in the program I played a soft, soothing song and asked the group to again think about the spiritual experiences they had had in going to the temple. This time the responses flowed from several individuals. Again, I think most of those in attendance understood and agreed with the point that some music invites the Spirit in.

In general, certain types of people are either attracted to or repelled by different types of music. To demonstrate this, I made a demonstration tape with short excerpts from various types of music, including classical, LDS hymns, silly children's songs, non-LDS gospel songs, soft rock, country western, hard rock, bluegrass, and Primary songs.

After playing a short excerpt from a song in each category, I ask members of my audience to describe in general terms, the type of people who listen to each particular type of music. This exercise has limitations, of course. Though a group of people who enjoy a certain type of music may, as a whole, behave in a certain way, individuals who enjoy the same type music may differ. With this in mind, think about each of the categories of music and ask yourself:

1. How do you think the people would dress who enjoy this type of music?

2. Do you think the people who enjoy this music drink alcoholic beverages, smoke, or use illegal drugs?

3. Would you be surprised if the people who listened to this type music were immoral? Do you think they are active church goers? Do you feel that, as a group, they read scriptures or say their prayers?

4. How would you generally describe the type of person who enjoys this type of music?

The question really becomes this: Are people who listen to certain categories of music perceived as acting a certain way? Both teens and adults are quick to point out that a particular type of music is associated with use of tobacco and beer, or another one is associated with drugs and rebellion, while another one is associated with older people.

THE CHALLENGE OF MODERN MUSIC 99

If these observations are correct, then ask yourself this question: Is a certain type of person attracted to this kind of music, or does exposure to the music create that type of person? Think of music you listen to the most and ask yourself what kind of person others would expect you to be. What about the music your children listen to? Are you or your children really that type of person? Do you share similar ideas with the group associated with your favorite music? Is there a correlation between actual behavior patterns and the type of behavior associated with a person's favorite music?

Music can change our moods and sometimes even our actions. In demonstrating this point to youth groups, I play short excerpts from three different songs. After hearing each song, members of the group are asked what they wanted to do when the song was playing. The real question is whether it influences their actual behavior.

The first is a very fast-paced, popular dance song. I ask the group what they feel like doing when they hear this song. The answer is almost always to dance or do something physical. The second song has a familiar, catchy melody with easy words to learn. The listeners point out that they want to sing along with this tune. The third song is a soft, mellow melody that they say makes them feel like relaxing, sleeping, studying, or meditating.

When we consider that the average American listens to almost thirteen hundred hours of music each year, it would seem wise to choose music that will build our spirits up rather than tear them down.

I wonder if parents are aware of the types of music their children are listening to. I'll never forget the surprise I received while trying to teach my own children the importance of music and the influence it can have in our lives. When I read that a famous hard-rock group was appearing at our local civic center, I decided to take my children to the area just to watch the people going to the concert. I expected the fans to drive up on motorcycles with knives and chains fastened to their belts, and that this would frighten our children into avoiding this type of music. Instead, I was startled to see mothers and fathers drive up in station wagons, vans, and cars and drop off well-dressed teenagers. Among them, unfortunately, were several LDS teens. Although it wasn't the lesson I had planned on my children's learning, I gleaned something from the night's activities. Many good children are listening to and supporting unworthy music, and many parents are not aware of the dangers of this kind of music. In fact, they are actually helping to support this bad influence by providing money for their children to purchase the record albums and attend the concerts.

As parents, we must expose ourselves and our children to good music in our homes if we are to counter the degrading music available in our society. If we do not provide our children with opportunities to hear worthy, uplifting music, then we shouldn't be surprised if they learn to enjoy the music they are being exposed to by their peers and society.

What can we do to counter the negative influence of music and turn it into a positive experience in our families? First, we need to realize that perhaps some family members may already be deeply attached to harmful music, and it will take an understanding spirit to work this situation out. Second, we must remember that if our family does not enjoy good music because of lack of exposure, the fault rests squarely on our shoulders. It is our responsibility to teach appreciation of good music, and if it has not happened yet, we can resolve to do better from now on.

In an attitude of cooperation and love, we can call our family together to discuss music, and let each of them express their ideas and opinion regarding this subject. The lines of communication must be kept open. Remember, relationships need to be maintained, so we must be very sensitive in dealing with this problem. We should try to remember how we felt about the music that was popular when we were young. To be accepted in the teenage society often requires at least some acquaintance with current music fads. To many young people, the music appears to be youthful, sophisticated, exciting, and harmless. But they should be reminded that society has undergone subtle but powerful changes in recent years. It has become increasingly more permissive in what is accepted in popular entertainment, including music. As the Lord's people, we must be willing to eliminate the inappropriate music from our homes. But, if we simply eliminate the music from our homes, we have only won a part of the battle. We also need to cultivate love for appropriate music. Only then will we have won the war.

Here are some suggestions to consider for your family council:

1. Buy a magazine that contains the words of the popular songs. As a family, review the words and discuss the messages. Ask questions: Why is this song popular? Is the artist trying to get us to live closer to the gospel or does it lure us farther from it?

2. Review with your family members their personal record and tape collections. Look at each of the record album covers, play excerpts from some of the songs, and discuss the messages. Are posters of musicians on the walls of any family member's bedroom walls? If so, discuss what is the attraction of that particular entertainer. If possible, find out what kind of moral values the favorite music groups have.

3. In a spirit of cooperation, establish some rules and limits. You may want to limit the amount of time spent listening to the radio or allow only certain stations to be played. Remember that we don't need to give up all popular music. Much of it is still good. But we must be willing to control our listening habits to avoid spiritually harmful music.

I have found the following suggestions helpful in providing a deeper appreciation for good music. I hope some will be useful to your family.

1. *Build a music library.* It is hard to appreciate good music if you don't have good music to listen to. Set up a program to acquire music for your home on a regular basis. Include music of several different types to provide a variety. If you need help, ask a respected musician for advice on building a musical library to fit your family's needs and budget. A

good musical library is essential if families are to gain an appreciation of good music.

2. *Attend concerts.* Plan well in advance to attend a classical music concert with your family. Before the event, discuss the music that will be played, the life of the composer, the proper attire to be worn to the concert, and manners that should be used. After the concert, purchase records or tapes of the music that was played for your music library. Music seems to take on new meaning after you have heard it played live in concert.

3. *Learn to play a musical instrument.* Consider making it a family tradition that every family member play a musical instrument. Imagine the joy that can come from having a family band. And it seems hypocritical to encourage your children to develop their musical talents if we as parents refuse to do the same. Learning to play a musical instrument may help a child in many ways. *USA Today* reported the following: "Want to get to the top in politics or business? Musical training can be a big help, say most Congressmen and Fortune 500 Chief Executive Officers. Ninety percent of more than 1000 C.E.O.'s and Congressmen interviewed by the McDonald's fast food chain said playing a musical instrument as a child helped them develop 'character and leadership skills.' "[2]

4. *Write an original family song.* Sing it at family home evening or on other special occasions. If you lack creativity, write words to a familiar tune. When your children have special experiences, urge them to write their feelings in verse form and try to put music to the words.

5. *Carry a hymn book in the car.* When traveling for a long distance, make it a tradition to learn new songs and to sing everyone's favorites. If you have younger children, take along a children's songbook as well.

6. *Analyzing music.* Spend an evening listening to several different kinds of music, such as pop, jazz, bluegrass, classical, and country western. Discuss with your family the following: Why do you believe the song was written? What is the message? Does it make you feel good or make you want to be a better

person? What makes the song appealing or unappealing to our society or to your family? Discuss the elements of each song, such as lyrics, harmony, tempo, and melody. Have family members describe the effect each song has on them personally.

7. *Discuss and review hymns.* Select some of your favorite hymns and spend an evening learning about the composers and lyricists. What are the backgrounds of the individuals? Were they trained musicians? What inspired them to write the hymn?[3] Discuss why the Church places emphasis on music in our meetings and activities.

8. *Learn what the scriptures say.* Spend an evening reading and discussing all the scriptural references to music you can find. Search also for statements by the latter-day prophets. Consider why music has appealed to the Lord's people in all recorded history, and why you think the Lord approves of it.

9. *Tape record your family's music.* Make tapes of your family singing and playing musical instruments. Review the tapes occasionally and note progress being made. Be sure that you keep these tapes for your personal and family histories.

10. *Play "Name That Tune."* Divide your family into teams and choose a leader for each group. Play a few notes of a song and then allow one team to attempt to guess the title. If no one gets it right, turn it over to the other team. Keep adding notes until one of the teams answers correctly. When the song has been identified, sing the song together as a family.

11. *Play "Continue Singing."* Select a leader. Then divide the rest of the family into two teams. The leader will sing the first line of a familiar song. The first team will confer, then have its leader sing the second line. If the line is correct, the team wins five points. Then the leader will sing the first line of another song, and the other team will try to identify the second line. Continue alternating between teams until one team has twenty-five points and wins the game.

12. *Play "Musical Hash."* Select a leader, who will prepare a list of familiar song titles with the letters of each word scrambled. Give a copy of the list to each player. The first person to unscramble all the titles wins the game.

There are many things we can do to help our families learn to appreciate good music, if we are willing to invest the time and effort.

Recently, I taught a class on the martyrdom of Joseph Smith and the beginnings of the Church's exodus to the West. At the conclusion, I played the tape of a song titled "Joseph." As we listened, I could see the effect the song was having upon the class members. Almost everyone in the class was wiping away tears. The spirit and emotion were so strong that the young woman who gave the closing prayer had to struggle to speak the words. We had planned to have an activity after class, but one student said, "It just doesn't seem appropriate now." It was one of those special experiences that you do not forget. It was an experience brought on by beautiful music.

Yes, music can have a very powerful influence in our lives. Let us make sure that in our homes and among our children, this influence is uplifting and good.

NOTES

1. Edward J. Whetmore, *Mediamerica: Form, Content, and Consequence of Mass Communication* (Belmont, California: Wadsworth Publishing Co., 1985), p. 135.

2. *USA Today*, January 19, 1987, section D, p. 1.

3. For background information on *Hymns of The Church of Jesus Christ of Latter-day Saints*, 1985, see Karen Lynn Davidson, *Our Latter-day Hymns: The Stories and the Messages* (Salt Lake City: Deseret Book, 1988).

CHAPTER 8

PROTECTING OUR COMMUNITIES

It would be comforting to think that our responsibility regarding obscenity ends with our own families, but this is not the case. We must also be concerned about our neighbors and do all in our power to help protect them from the evils of our day. President Spencer W. Kimball said the following concerning this duty: "We hope that our parents and leaders will not tolerate pornography. It is really garbage, but today is peddled as normal and satisfactory food. Many writers seem to take delight in polluting the atmosphere with it. Seemingly, it cannot be stopped by legislation. There is a link between pornography and the low, sexual drives and perversions.... We pray with our Lord that we may be kept from being in the world. It is sad that decent people are thrown into a filthy area of mental and spiritual pollution. We call upon all our people to do all in their power to offset this ugly revolution."[1]

A few years ago in a priesthood lesson on our responsibilities as citizens, the teacher asked us what our responsibility was toward the obscenity that had become so prevalent in our society. One brother expressed the opinion that we just needed to worry about our own families and not get involved in this type of problem in our society, because it's a free country and the peddlers of smut have their freedom of speech and should not be interfered with. Another pointed out that the U.S. Supreme Court has ruled in several cases that obscenity is not protected under the first amendment to the Constitution and that obscenity could be defined according to contemporary community standards. I wondered to myself, Where does the truth lie? What is our responsibility? What have our modern prophets said on this subject?

Later I found that President Kimball had commented on this very subject several times. On one occasion he asked the same question we had been discussing and added two other questions: "Should people be free to infect society with obscene pictures and vulgar articles and flaunt corruption before children and others? Why should a few be granted freedom from restraint when many are fettered by the ugliness to which they are exposed?"[2] President Kimball gave us the answers in many general conference talks. Here are two examples: "Important as it is, building stronger homes is not enough in the fight against rising permissiveness. We therefore urge Church members as citizens to lift their voices, to join others in unceasingly combatting, in their communities and beyond, the inroads of pornography and the general flaunting of permissiveness."[3] "Teach your children to avoid smut as the plague it is. As citizens, join in the fight against obscenity in your communities. Do not be lulled into inaction by the pornographic profiteers who say that to remove obscenity is to deny people the rights of free choice. Do not let them masquerade licentiousness as liberty. Precious souls are at stake — souls that are near and dear to each of us."[4]

After much discussion that day in priesthood meeting, our group came to general consensus that obscenity is really not protected by law and that we have a responsibility to fight it in our community. Then one of the brethren said he was thankful to live in an area that didn't have a problem with obscenity. I pointed out that not only did we have a problem in our area, but that pornographic magazines were available at a convenience store within a mile of the chapel, and that all of the video rental shops in town carried triple-X-rated movies that anyone could check out. Several older brethren couldn't believe that this was happening, but some of the younger ones finally convinced them it was true.

Before the lesson ended, we resolved to try to do what we could to help eliminate the problem in our area. Since I was the only one in attendance that day who lived within the city limits, it was decided that I should try to do something about obscenity in the city, and the rest of the group would attempt to get rid of it outside the city limits. Knowing that almost all of the offending businesses were located in the city, I wondered what I had gotten into.

During the next week I did nothing to try to solve the problem. At church on Sunday I learned that some of the brethren had turned over the assignment to their wives, who in turn had had some success. After a few friendly phone calls to store owners, ministers of other faiths, and the added impact of a threatened boycott of their stores by church members who usually traded in their stores, most of the managers had removed obscene materials within a few days. The owner of the largest privately owned convenience store removed the offending magazines from all his branch stores because of one phone call.

That night I called our mayor and asked him if an ordinance against obscenity hadn't been passed in our city. He replied that yes, a very detailed ordinance made it unlawful to sell, rent, display, lend, give away, show, advertise, or distribute any obscene magazine or movie within the city limits. I asked him why the law was not being enforced, citing examples of several video rental stores in the city that were renting triple-X-rated movies. He replied that someone needed to make a complaint that the law was not being enforced before the city could officially act on it. I said, "Then I complain." He informed me that I had to appear before the city council the next Tuesday night with proof that the films were actually available and that the owners of the video shops would rent them. We decided that it would be even better if I could find a minor who would check out the movies, since the ordinance had even more specific provisions pertaining to those under eighteen.

That night I hung up the phone wondering what I had just agreed to do. What had started in the priesthood class as a simple challenge had now gotten much bigger than anything I wanted to be involved in. But the following Tuesday my ten-year-old son and the seventeen-year-old daughter of one of our ward members walked into a video rental shop and rented two of the most controversial and financially successful XXX-movies of all time. They handed the videocassettes to me, and I drove directly across the street to city hall with the evidence in hand. (I was praying that the city leaders would not want to view the films, but would recognize the titles as obscenity because of the publicity the movies had received in the nationwide press. My prayers were answered because they never asked to see the films, and we returned the unopened cases the next day.)

As I took my seat, I felt the cold stare of a man whom I knew to be the owner of the largest video rental chain in the area. The mayor came over to shake my hand, and I asked him what the other man was doing at this meeting. He said, "He heard you were going to be here to make a presentation on obscenity," he said, "so he came to hear what you had to say." I suddenly became frightened and also tempted to get up and leave without making a complaint. But a quick silent prayer gave me the courage I needed to stay.

After disposing of other business matters, the mayor finally stood up and said that "a concerned citizen, Randal Wright, would like to express some concerns he has regarding our city." As I stood up and started to talk, to my own surprise my first words were that I felt we needed to make an effort to attract a good triple-X movie theater to our city. I then paused and listened to the shocked reaction of the mayor, council, and the observers of this very conservative Bible-belt city. The mayor asked me to repeat my statement, which I did. He then asked me to explain why I thought we should seek to get a triple-X movie theater in our city. I replied, "It's not that I really want to see this happen. I am totally opposed to it. But I would much prefer an adult movie house to the situation we have now." I then explained that we now had adult movie houses all over our city, but they were located in people's homes. "We have adults as well as minors checking out triple-X-rated movies from video shops and playing them in their own homes, in clear violation of the city law," I said.

I then related how my ten-year-old son and a seventeen-year-old friend had just checked out two very controversial pornographic movies within five hundred feet of city hall. Many in the audience gasped when I gave the titles of these movies. "At least," I pointed out, "adult movie theaters are controlled and monitored by police, and they do not allow minors to enter. That's more than I can say for our present situation. As it is, we now have absolutely no control over obscenity in our city." Then I read the city ordinance and the state law regarding obscene materials and asked the council to please enforce these laws that were on the books.

There was complete silence in the room. Then the owner of the video-store chain stood up and began contending with me. He said that his business did not rent to minors, and that he had over $150,000 invested in adult movies and could not afford to lose this investment. He spoke of people's rights under the first amendment and used many other arguments. When he finished I said, "Sir, would you do anything that you knew would harm the adults or the youth of our city?" He said, "Of course not. I would never do anything to harm the people in this area." Next, I held out a stack of papers and said, "I hold in my hand over fifteen hundred references to research that links obscenity to antisocial behavior and sex crimes and warns of the dangers to those involved." He said that he was unaware of the research, but repeated that his firm did not rent adult films to minors and that it was his right to rent such films. I then asked him, "Sir, at what age does your mind grow a 'smut filter'?" He asked me to repeat the question. "At what age does your mind grow a 'smut filter'? Is it age sixteen, eighteen, or twenty-one? At what age does the human mind filter out obscene material to the point that it doesn't have any effect on you?" He said that he didn't understand the question. Suddenly a man who identified himself as a church youth leader stood up and said he understood the question, because a lot of his time was spent counseling young people who had been damaged by obscenity. Another person stood up and then another, each voicing objections that the city was not enforcing the laws and ordinances on obscenity. At this point the mayor called for a closed-door session and we were asked to leave. Several people expressed their support to me as we walked out to our cars.

The next morning as I walked into seminary, a student asked if I had seen the front page of the morning newspaper. I hadn't, so he showed me the headline: "CITY COUNCIL OUTLAWS SELLING OF PORNOGRAPHY." The article stated that the city council had voted unanimously to enforce and even expand the current obscenity laws. After a two-week grace period, all obscene magazines and movies were to be out of our city limits.

From that day on, the law has been enforced. It is not possible to buy or rent any obscene movie in our city. Several businesses that rented both good and bad movies were forced to close, and I regret that. I also received several calls from individuals who did not agree with my stand. But overall the people have rallied around the law and are proud of the better image our city enjoys. I have found through personal experience that we can have an influence in our families and our communities when we follow the words of our prophets.

The *Church News* some time ago presented several excellent ideas to help us have a positive impact in our communities, including these:

    1. Organize with like-minded citizens in your community.

    2. Become informed about pornography. What is it? What are the existing laws? Who are the government and civic officials who can make a difference? What legal remedies are available?

3. Inventory the pornography in your neighborhood and community. Include TV programs, videocassettes, magazines, newspapers, movies, bookstores, and video rental stores.

4. Share information with friends, neighbors, other church members, other groups, and citizens' committees. Consider initiating a petition.

5. Work together to contact owners of offending businesses and ask for cooperation. In person and in writing, courteously encourage the owners to put questionable materials out of sight and stop selling pornography. Send a copy of your correspondence to the headquarters of each business. If the practice persists, start a campaign to have others write letters also.

6. Refuse to buy from a business owner who will not cooperate.

7. Write letters to local newspapers. Visit them alone or with a delegation.

8. Write and visit city, county, state, and federal officials. Ask them to enforce existing obscenity laws.

9. Evaluate other legal remedies with the help of an able attorney.

10. If needed, ask for passage of new laws to deal with the situation.

11. Contact radio and TV stations. Write letters and visit station owners, managers, or editors alone or with a delegation. Share your facts. Ask for cooperation.

12. If you are a citizen of the United States, write to the President, the U.S. Attorney General, senators, and congressmen. Write to the U.S. Postmaster General to encourage enforcement of statutes forbidding use of the mail to transmit pornographic materials.

It is our duty and responsibility to teach not only our own families the dangers of obscenity, but our communities as well. We must become more involved because of the precious souls at stake. How can we expect to have success teaching the gospel message to people who have been immersed in obscenity? Obscene materials will desensitize them to the truth. In the

Book of Mormon, Jacob felt not only a responsibility to teach his own family, but also to teach others. He said: "And we did magnify our office unto the Lord, taking upon us the responsibility, answering the sins of the people upon our own heads if we did not teach them the word of God with all diligence; wherefore, by laboring with our might their blood might not come upon our garments; otherwise their blood would come upon our garments, and we would not be found spotless at the last day." (Jacob 1:19.)

What is our office unto the Lord? Do we not have a civic as well as spiritual responsibility? Our prophets have repeatedly said that we do. Our cities and our nation are a part of the environment in which our families dwell. If our citizens are not informed, it is our responsibility to inform them of the acts and dangers that will bring upon them shattered lives and misery.

When our two sons were younger, I took them and their eight-year-old cousin Max to the Southeast Texas State Fair. We had a good time riding all the rides and looking at the exhibits. As we were preparing to go home, I asked the boys if they wanted some cotton candy to eat in the car. They did, so I bought each of them a large bag. As we drove home, I could tell they were enjoying the treat. Max looked especially funny with cotton candy all over his hands, mouth, nose, and chin. I was just about to tell him he needed to clean his face, when he said, "I sure am glad I finished that cotton candy before I got home!" When I asked Max why, he said that his mother had told him before he left home that he couldn't have any cotton candy. I debated whether or not I should tell him about the candy all over his face, but I finally decided to let him go in the house with the evidence still there, to answer to his mother for being disobedient.

I'm afraid some of us are going to be a lot like Max when we stand before the judgment bar of Christ. Some may think they are going to get away with disobeying our Heavenly Father while on earth. Some may think they will get away with watching inappropriate movies or allowing family members to do so without any negative consequences. Others may refuse to follow the living prophet's counsel or assume they will never have to answer for not becoming involved in our communities to fight this increasing threat. But in the end none of us will be able to escape giving an accounting for ourselves at the judgment bar. Some will find, as Max did when he faced his mother, that we will not be able to fool our eternal judges with our earthly actions, because the evidence will be apparent by either our clean or unclean appearances. Let us do our duty so we can return to our Father in heaven clean, having obeyed all of his commandments.

NOTES

1. Spencer W. Kimball, "God Will Not Be Mocked," *Ensign*, November 1974, p. 7.

2. "Stand by Your Guns," address delivered at the institute of religion adjacent to the Utah State University campus, Logan, Utah, October 14, 1966.

3. "The Foundations of Righteousness," *Ensign*, November 1977, p. 45.

4. "A Report and a Challenge," *Ensign*, November 1976, p. 6.

CHAPTER 9

HELPING YOUTH STAY MORALLY CLEAN

A few years ago two of my seminary students attended a conference on rape prevention at our city's civic center. Many experts spoke and provided safety tips to help young women avoid being sexually assaulted. The ideas included always going in teams to public places, wearing modest clothing, not accepting gifts from strangers, and above all, not getting into a car with a stranger, no matter how pleasant the individual or the invitation may be. The conference leaders then presented statistics related to the dangers in our area and described in detail some of the consequences of not following the safety precautions.

My students listened very carefully to the presentations. In fact, they listened so well that they became terrified and were afraid to walk back to their car, parked some distance from the civic center. They stood in front of the building and debated whether or not they should call their parents to come and pick them up. At that point, a man and woman, who were total strangers to them, walked up and asked what the problem was. When the girls explained that they were afraid to walk to their car alone, the man invited them to get into his car so he could drive them to their car. What do you think they did? The girls, relieved with this proposal, actually got into the car with two people they had never seen or met before. Now luckily this is not a horror story, as it could have been, because the man did drive them to their car and they returned home safely. The next morning at seminary the girls told us about the conference and their experience. It wasn't until they heard the comments from the other students that they realized they had done exactly what the experts had told them not to do when they had gotten into the car with two strangers.

Sometimes parents are a lot like these students. They hear the counsel repeatedly about protecting their children from the dangers of immorality, and then, when the danger comes, they feel perfectly at ease letting their children enter dangerous situations without so much as a warning. Several years ago a mother told me that she had agreed to let her daughter celebrate the end of the school year by spending three days at a lakeside resort with the daughter's nonmember steady boyfriend and his parents. I thought of how dangerous this trip could be for this young girl and tried tactfully to point this fact out to the mother. However, she let me know quickly that she trusted her daughter and that she was not going to force her own ideas or concerns onto her child. I thought to myself that this was like trusting a small child to play on a busy freeway. I also thought about how I trust my children too, but I don't trust Satan, and when we put ourselves in his territory, we have no promise of safety—but I said nothing. Nine months later this teenage girl was a new mother.

When our daughter Natalie started kindergarten, she was happy for the first week and was always the first one up and ready in the morning. By the second week, I noticed that she was still excited but was no longer the first one up. She would just as soon stay home to play with her little sister. By the third week, she wasn't excited at all. One morning when I told her it was time to get up, she didn't even open her eyes. "Don't want to go to school," she told me. I said, "Natalie, you need to get up and get ready for school." She said even slower, "Not going to school."

What should I have done? I didn't want to force my daughter to do something against her will and thus take away her free agency. But I also didn't want to have a kindergarten drop-out, because I knew that one day she would thank me for encouraging her to get an education. So I decided to try to reason with her. First I stated that our government had made a state law requiring young children to attend school. This had no effect on her whatsoever. I then told her that her parents had gone to school, her older brothers and sister were going to school now, and we expected her to continue to go. She was not impressed. Next I told her that she needed to go because it was a family rule and goal that all our family go to school. This helped somewhat, but she still wasn't convinced. Finally after attempting several other tactics, I told her that if she would get up and go to school, I would buy her a big ice cream cone that night. Now I was talking her language. She now had a goal, so she got up and happily went to school. And since that day, she has never complained again about going to school. She was able to make her own choice, and her free agency was preserved.

Without goals and encouragement from parents and leaders, most youths would avoid almost anything that is hard to do. In today's permissive society, staying morally clean is very hard to do. It takes effort on the part of both parents and children to accomplish this goal.

Children need to be able to make correct decisions on their own. And helping them achieve this should be the goal of all parents. But as parents, we also need to make sure they are protected until they are old enough and mature enough to make these decisions. They need freedom, but they also need protection. It takes the promptings of the Spirit to know when to let them go—and when to step in and try to protect them. I've made it a goal and even a rule that in our home we should always try to be where we are supposed to be, when we are supposed to be there, and doing what we are supposed to be doing. Weekend trips to a resort with a boyfriend are forbidden, no matter how much trust we have in our daughters. This is not where they should be. On the other hand, they should be at youth conferences, at seminary, and at activities sponsored by the Young Women and Aaronic Priesthood quorums. There should be no questions about whether they will go to such programs or activities any more than whether or not Natalie should go to school.

Many will say, "What about letting them make their own decisions? We can't *force* them to do good." No, but there are still plenty of opportunities for decisions and free agency, even when they are always where they are supposed to be. For instance, we may ask a child what he wants to wear to church, but not *if* he wants to go to church. Or does he want to take a camera to youth conference, not *if* he wants to attend. If children are allowed to make all their own decisions, with no counsel, what is the purpose of parents?

Suppose your teenage daughter comes in one day and shows you a pillowcase a friend has given her. She explains that this friend told her that if she jumped off a high building, the pillowcase would act as a parachute and protect her fall. She then asks for permission to jump off a tall building using the pillowcase as a parachute. Would you allow your daughter to try this feat? What would you say if she begged you? How about if she promised to keep her room clean for a year? What if she said you could trust her? We all know what your answer would be, no matter what argument she used. It would be *no*, under *no* circumstances. And then, as a loving parent, you would explain why you could not allow her to do this.

Yet, some teenagers come in with plans, like a weekend at a lake resort or long evenings alone with their boyfriend or girlfriend, and many parents say yes. Sometimes the consequences of these decisions are disastrous. If our children are going to remain safe and morally clean, they need to be taught the dangers and to have some safety guides and rules set by their parents to help protect them. We must be concerned about where they go, what they are doing, whom they are associating with, and when they will be home, if they are to be safe.

Some may question whether it is even possible to get children through their teenage years totally moral. Others may believe that parents can do nothing, and that luck is responsible if teenagers remain morally clean. I don't believe that this is true. Young people can stay morally clean, but it takes work on both the parents' and the children's part.

I'll never forget the missionary farewell of a young man named Eric Wold. He had done everything he was expected to do in the Church. I had observed his family and knew that it was no accident that Eric was going on a mission. They had expectations, goals, rules, and plenty of encouragement for their children. But Eric was even more outstanding than I had at first thought. When his father talked, we learned of an experience in Eric's life that really made us proud of him. After high school he applied to work at a convenience store, and before he was hired, he had to take a lie-detector test. His father was with him when the man who had administered this test came out with the results. The man said, "Are you Eric's father?" He replied that he was. The man then said, "Well, I just wanted to tell that you have a fine boy here. I've been giving these tests for thirty-six years, and Eric is the *first* person who has ever answered no to all the questions." Tears came to my eyes as I thought about this young man who had attended a high school with two thousand students, a school where he and his sister were the only Latter-day Saints enrolled, and who had stayed completely clean and virtuous in the face of all the many temptations.

How can we keep our children morally clean? What are some of the things that successful families do to produce such fine and moral children? Here are some things I have learned about helping our families stay morally clean.

1. One of the best protections youth can have against immorality is good self-esteem. If children feel good about them-

selves, they have a much better chance of remaining virtuous. On the other hand, when children feel insecure or bad about themselves, the chances of their being immoral increase dramatically. We need to constantly encourage and build up our children so they feel good about themselves. One of the best ways for a child to achieve high self-esteem is through excelling at something. A child who can play a musical instrument, sing, participate in sports, debate or earn good grades usually has a higher self-esteem than one who accomplishes little in life. But such achievements take work, and many children do not have the drive to achieve without constant encouragement from their parents. And when things go wrong and children want to quit or give up, parents must be there to build them back up and give them the courage to keep trying. We all have days when nothing seems to go quite right.

When I was in the ninth grade, I wanted to play basketball on our church team. Every day after school, I would go down to the outdoor basketball court at the church and practice for several hours. Soon I could feel myself becoming better at the game, and my self-esteem increased until I felt I was really worth something as a player and as a person. Finally, the basketball season came around, and our ward began to practice as a team. Our coach (who had never played organized basketball before, so he knew very little about the game) gave us a pep talk before our first game. He said, "Okay, men, if you want to win this game, you are going to have to give the ball to Randal and let him shoot. If he misses, get the rebound, pass it back to him, and let him shoot again." I thought to myself, *This coach is a genius.* I was very eager to show off my ability.

Our ward was out in the country, and we didn't have a lot of money as the city wards did. None of our players had basketball shorts or jerseys, and only two had basketball shoes. Two others went barefoot, and I wore my scuffed-up Sunday shoes, which I also wore Monday through Saturday. One of the first things the coach of the opposing team did was to tell me to take off my hard-soled shoes before I messed up the gym floor, so I now became the third member of our team playing barefoot. The opposing team all had basketball shoes and matching uniforms with their names printed on their jerseys.

When the game started, I did what my coach had told me to do. On offensive plays I dribbled the ball down the court and shot every time I got near the basket. If my teammates got a rebound, they would pass the ball back to me and I would shoot again. I continued to shoot the ball over and over again, just as the coach had told me to do, but the longer the game went on, the more my feet hurt and the bigger the blisters on them became. Finally, with about two minutes left in the game, the coach took me out. The first time my replacement got the ball, he scored two points. The final score that day was 52 to 2. My replacement had scored our only two points. Needless to say, I was humiliated, and I didn't want to go to church that Sunday to face those who had watched the game. It's times like these, when we are down and discouraged and our self-esteem is low, that Satan likes to work on us. What a great protection it is to have a parent say, "Son, just because you had a bad day, it doesn't make you a bad person or a failure. Get back out there and keep practicing, and you'll do better next time."

2. Another protection against immorality, one that is closely related to high self-esteem, is to set goals. I'm continually amazed at how many graduating high school seniors don't even know what they will be doing in the fall after graduation. Setting the right kind of goals and striving to achieve them can help children stay morally clean. But they can't wait until they are caught up in a situation to set their goals. They need to set them while they are very young. I've found that most children need guidance in setting the kinds of goals that will help protect them in their dating years. I have tried to help my own children set some of their life's goals when they turn eight years old, the time when they become responsible for their own actions. At that age, they are also young enough that most of them have not really been tempted in any moral areas.

When my son Nolan was eight years old, we sat down together and helped him set his goals. Then we typed them on colored paper, put the paper in a frame, and hung it on his bedroom wall, so he could see his goals every day of his life. Following are the goals he set:

I will study the scriptures every day.
I will pray to Heavenly Father both morning and night.
I will be a full tithe payer.
I will strive to achieve 100% attendance at church, school, seminary, etc.
I will always keep physically fit.
I will try to be a good sport.
I will learn to play the piano and one other musical instrument.
I will never break the Word of Wisdom.
I will become an Eagle Scout.
I will be a faithful priesthood holder.
I will not begin dating until age 16, and then only in groups; no single dating until after my mission.
I will be diligent in school, church, and other responsibilities.
I will always stay morally clean.
I will strive never to think I'm better than others.
I will graduate from seminary.
I will strive to understand and develop every talent with which the Lord has blessed me.
I will always keep a personal journal.
I will always dress modestly.
I will never turn down a church assignment.
I will strive to develop a good sense of humor and look for the positive in life.
I will fill an honorable full-time mission.
I will graduate from college.
I will be married in the temple for time and all eternity.

After these goals were typed, Nolan signed his name at the bottom of the paper with the date they were set. If he will consistently work on these goals, I believe he will be able to build an almost impenetrable barrier against immorality. We will do all we can to help support him in each of these goals.

3. If children are to take their goals seriously, they also

need some kind of accountability regarding them. This can be done through a monthly interview. The first Sunday of every month, we take down our children's goal sheets and use them as the basis for interviews. We discuss each goal and give encouragement and counsel on how to achieve it. This interview is also an excellent time to teach children about moral issues and answer any questions they may have. President Spencer W. Kimball said: "The home is the teaching situation [for sex education]. Every father should talk to his son, every mother to her daughter. Then it would leave them totally without excuse should they ignore the counsel they have received."[1]

If our children knew they would have consistent and effective interviews on a monthly basis, I believe that much of the immorality in the Church would be eliminated. Interviews should be conducted with love and should always begin with prayer. In teaching your children and asking them to give an account of their progress on their personal goals, you may occasionally wish to ask them to imagine that they are five years older than they actually are, and to participate in role-playing situations they may face five years from now. If they can determine a course of action early, they will not have to make decisions when a difficult situation actually presents itself in the future.

In our family, we have started several traditions that I believe can help keep our children on a safe path if followed consistently:

1. We give each of our children a kiss before they go to bed. This tradition, if it is started early and kept up through the teenage years, has many benefits. It lets the children know that they are loved, and this in turn helps build their self-esteem. It allows us to look into the children's eyes on a daily basis. If something is going wrong in their lives, we should be able to detect it early and take appropriate action. And a good-night kiss can also be a deterrent against drinking, smoking, and drug use by the children.

2. We believe that parents should wait up for their children when they go out, no matter what time they come in, so they

can discuss the evening's activities. This discussion should be done with genuine interest and not be an interrogation. Such a discussion can help us find out what problems our children are having and allow us to help them correct the problems in the early stages. The mother of one of my best friends in high school always waited up for her son to discuss his night's activities, no matter what time he came home. He later told me that he had been tempted several times to be immoral during his earlier dating years, but the knowledge that mother would always be waiting up for him was an effective protection and deterrent. This practice is so simple that one would think everyone would want to use it. Unfortunately, many parents disagree. For those who do disagree, these questions may be asked: How much sleep will you lose if your child is immoral? Would you rather lose a little sleep now or a lot of sleep later?

3. While attending Brigham Young University, I heard of another tradition from one of my professors. His own father has given each of his children a father's blessing every year on their birthdays. Although this professor now has eight children of his own, he still goes to his father once a year for his blessing. I liked this idea so well that I began it in my own family. To this day our five children have each received a father's blessing every year on their birthday. One of the things I always bless them with is the strength and determination to stay morally clean for the coming year. A special father's blessing could also be given at the beginning of the dating years for further protection. Let us never underestimate the power of the priesthood in helping to keep our youth morally clean.

If we are to help protect our children from immorality, we also need to establish some dating rules before they are old enough to date. If rules are implemented in a family early, there should be no questions when the dating years actually arrive. But if we wait until our children have already started dating and then try to establish rules, the rules will be much more difficult to implement.

The following rules are suggested as a strong deterrent in preventing youth from falling into immorality. All are based on the teachings of our prophets.

1. No dating until age 16.
2. No single dating until high school graduation for girls and after missions for boys.
3. No steady dating until high school graduation for girls and after missions for boys.
4. No dating nonmembers or unworthy members of the Church.

President Kimball said: "Dating—and especially steady dating in the early teens—is most hazardous. It distorts the whole picture of life. It deprives the youth of worthwhile and rich experiences; it limits friendships; it reduces the acquaintance which can be so valuable in selecting a partner for time and eternity. Steady dating is the source of much evil. The casual relationship grows rapidly into intimacies, develops heavy temptations, and stirs passions far beyond the ability of most young people to cope with."[2]

I believe that the four dating rules suggested above, if followed carefully, would eliminate much of the immorality in the Church today. But parents must have the courage to implement these rules and then insure that they are strictly followed.

Recently I discussed these rules with a long-time bishop. He made an interesting observation: "Of the dating-age youths I have interviewed who have followed the rules, to my knowledge not one has been immoral." On the other hand, he said that almost all of those teenagers who had freedom in their dating experiences with no rules at all had immorality problems. This same view was verified a short time later by a nationally known LDS family researcher who had just completed a major government research project on teen pregnancy. He said that the teenagers who had no dating rules had the highest percentage of premarital sex, while those who had strict dating rules had the lowest occurrences of premarital sex. And yet even with such evidence, many parents still refuse to adopt any dating rules. I've heard several say, "We don't need these rules. They are too strict. Besides, I trust my children." To all such responses I say, "I trust my children too, but I don't trust Satan." When we allow our children to place themselves in situations where our prophets have warned that they should not be, we are permitting them to go into Satan's territory, and he almost always wins on his own turf.

Finally, we need to control our use of various media if our families are to remain morally clean. Inappropriate magazines, TV, movies, and music can stir up lust that will nullify everything else we may teach our children. Satan desires our children and will do whatever he can to try to tempt them to be immoral. But with carefully planned goals and rules and a lot of prayer, we can eliminate much of this evil influence and help keep our children morally clean. As parents, we must be prepared and willing to make any effort necessary to counter the temptations they will face. It can be done!

NOTES

1. "God Will Not Be Mocked," *Ensign*, November 1974, p. 7.
2. "Save the Youth of Zion," *Improvement Era*, September 1965, p. 763.

CHAPTER 10

"INSPIRE THEM TO GREATNESS"

Several years ago a friend commented that he was tired of hearing the same subjects taught repeatedly at church meetings, such as tithing, missionary work, family home evening, keeping a journal, and food storage. He asked why the church didn't move on and emphasize some different topics. We talked about a few good reasons why such topics were constantly emphasized, including the fact that so many converts coming into the Church need to hear the basics and that some people are not living even the basics and need to be constantly reminded of their duties. My friend said that he understood those points, but he still thought we needed to move on to some deeper subjects for those who had been in the Church for years.

As I drove home that night, I wondered, why doesn't the Church move on to deeper subjects? Aren't we already doing the things asked of us, and don't we need further enlightenment? That night, I imagined myself at the judgment bar and Christ telling me I would be judged only for the last year of my life and only on the basic principles that our leaders have taught us over and over. I thought how easy for me this imaginary judgment was going to be, and wished that our real judgment would be that easy. Then I thought about some basic questions I might be asked, and I sat down and wrote them down. Here is what I wrote:

1. Have you said your personal and family prayers every day for the past 365 days?

2. Have you held a family home evening every week for the past 52 weeks?

3. Have you done your home teaching or visiting teaching every month for the past 12 months?

4. Have you read the scriptures every day for the past 365 days?

5. Have you kept a personal journal regularly for the past year?

6. Have you worked consistently on your genealogy for the past year?

7. Have you attended or read the reports of all the sessions of general conference for the past year?

8. Have you been to the temple regularly for the past year?

9. Have you consistently tried to do missionary work during the past year?

10. Have you obtained or maintained a year's supply of food and supplies over the last year, including raising a garden?

Bonus: Are you caring for your physical body through proper nutrition and a regular exercise program?

How would you answer these questions? Are you, like my friend, ready to move on to some of the more difficult questions? Or do you need to continue working on some of these basic principles? Now, actually reaching the celestial kingdom will require much more than answering these few simple questions. But we might all do well to ask ourselves, how am I really doing as a parent? Could my family achieve more if they followed my example in every way? Do we know who we are and where we are going in life? If not, this is a good time to start.

Being a parent is one of the most difficult, frustrating, and challenging—as well as fun-filled, rewarding, and joyful—experiences anyone could ever ask for. Our experience will usually depend on our attitude and the amount of effort we are willing to put forth. We must learn who *we* are and then teach our children who *they* are, if the experience is to be a positive one. But we should also remember that no Latter-day Saint parent is going to be totally successful every day. Some days we all struggle and become discouraged. But no matter how hard the task may be, we simply cannot give up if we want our families to do the things we were sent here to do. The key is to never give up. We must set the proper example, use every means possible to try to reach our children, and then persist and never give up.

We should also be constantly looking for ideas and ways to inspire our families. To do this, we need to avoid some of the extraneous distractions of our day, distractions that would keep us from pondering the things that will help our families most.

One of the best things that ever happened to me was that the radio in my car stopped working. One day as I drove to work in quietness, I discovered that without the distraction of the radio, I had time to ponder the things I need to do in my own life and to think of ways I might help others over whom I have stewardship. Now every day I set a goal or think about a problem and then try to come up with a solution before I arrive at work. For example, one of my seminary students said he saw nothing wrong with sampling a few grapes in the grocery store when he shopped. Most of the other students in class agreed and said that four or five grapes was such a small amount that it was not a big deal. After class, as I drove without distractions, I pondered this problem and prayed for guidance to help my students see that this view is definitely wrong. The next day I gave everyone in the class a handout headed as follows: "Thou Shalt Not Steal... Nor Do Anything Like unto It." (D&C 59:6).

Issue: Eating a few grapes at supermarket without paying for them.

Question: What's wrong with sampling the grapes while shopping?
Number of grapes sampled: 5.
Weight of 5 grapes: 1 ounce (average).
Cost of grapes per pound: $1.00.
Question: If grapes were sampled every day, what would be the loss to the store?

CASE 1
1 person
1 day = $.06 (1/16 pound of grapes)
1 year = $21.90 (21.9 pounds of grapes)

CASE 2
1 family (16 people)
1 day = $1.00
1 year = $365.00

CASE 3
City of Vidor, Texas (38,000 people)
1 day = $2,375
1 year = $866,875

CASE 4
State of Texas (15 million people)
1 day = $937,500
1 year = $342,187,500

CASE 5
United States (250 million people)
1 day = $15,625,000
1 year = $5,703,185,000

CASE 6
Worldwide (6 billion people)
1 day = $375,000,000
1 year = $136,875,000,000

I pointed out that this amount of grapes sampled by one person may not seem significant, but if everyone in the city or the country did so, the results would be devastating. After reviewing the scriptural teachings regarding honesty, most of the students had a change of heart regarding the harm of taking a few grapes. We must constantly be on the alert for teaching moments with our children. But unless we take time to ponder, the opportunities will usually go by, and our families will be left without a stronger desire to be better.

After a stake assignment in a neighboring city several years ago, I came home to find my wife, Wendy, upset and frustrated. I asked her how the children had behaved at church, and she told me that they had been irreverent in sacrament meeting. Irreverence is not usually a problem in our family, so I gave my children a quick lecture and sent them on about their Sabbath day activities. Wendy, however, felt that the subject needed more attention, so we decided to devote our family home evening to reverence. During my quiet time in the car the next day, I tried to come up with a solution.

The lesson that night began in the usual manner—another message on why we should be reverent and what would happen the next time the children chose not to be reverent in church meetings. The children didn't seem particularly interested and began to fidget and look away. Then the lesson took on a new twist that our family will never forget.

I asked Nathan, who was eight, to go into another room for a few minutes, then return when called to tell the family a story he liked. While he was out of the room, I told the other three children that when he returned and began to tell his story, we would all talk, giggle, and fidget.

Nathan returned and began his story. He is an excellent storyteller and has won awards for his talent, so he thought this would be an easy assignment. Then he realized that no one was listening to him. Without his audience's attention, he began fumbling for words. Finally, totally frustrated, he sat down without finishing his tale.

When I asked him how this experience had made him feel, he hung his head and replied, "Really bad!"

Next we asked Nolan, who was seven, to leave the room. When he was invited back to tell us a story, he said, "I don't know any stories." He knew what was about to happen, and he wanted no part of it. We suggested a story to him and asked him to tell it to us. But when he tried to tell his story and we didn't pay attention, he burst into tears and said, "I can't do it! I can't talk when other people are talking!"

Here was the teaching moment I had hoped for. I explained, "Now you know how speakers and teachers feel when the people in the congregation or class are irreverent. They feel bad inside, just as you do now. They would like to just sit down and quit too. But they can't do that. They have to continue."

My children understood. We had all learned an important lesson.

In order to experience the positive side of this lesson, we then asked the other children to sit up straight, fold their arms, and look at Nathan as he told his story again. This time there was a dramatic difference. He did an excellent job, using facial expressions and hand gestures without stumbling on one word.

After the children had gone to bed that night, I felt proud of the lesson on reverence. They had truly learned something that night. But then a thought came strongly to me. The children had learned, but what about me? Did *I* know the meaning of the word *reverence*?

I thought about my past behavior. How many times had I whispered during church meetings and classes? How many times had I worked on talks or read during meetings? How many times had I interrupted others when they were speaking? Upon examining my own actions, I found I had not always looked at teachers or speakers when they were speaking to me, and I seldom expressed appreciation to the teacher, the speaker, or others for a job well done. I found that I needed to work on being more reverent as much as my children did.

Since that day our family has learned to enjoy our meetings and glean more from them than ever before. But that lesson was not learned until I had pondered the problem and asked for help. To help our families change undesirable behavior, we must constantly seek solutions and teaching moments. I am confident the Lord will show us the way to improve ourselves and to teach our families if we will only seek.

In a priesthood class I once attended, we discussed the need and the responsibility we all had to attend the temple. Because of the distance a few mentioned the financial sacrifice that it required to make a temple trip regularly. I considered this awhile and thought to myself, "You know, it's very strange what we can afford and what we can't." That evening, as I sat thinking of these comments, I wrote the following:

> It's amazing, isn't it? I mean, what we can afford and what we can't. I know that we should plan a regular temple

trip to renew our marriage covenants and do work for the dead, but maybe later. We just can't afford it now, with the payments due on our new car. And fast offerings—I just can't afford any more than I'm already giving. ("Honey, call the Joneses and see if they want to go eat steak and seafood Friday night after the game.") I realize my sons should have suits for church and our daughters better dresses, but times are hard. ("Who wants to go get treats tonight and play a few computer games?") Buy some spiritual music for the home? I'm going to get some soon, but I just spent my extra money on the top rock album. And good books, yes, I need more good things to read in the home, but my sports magazine subscription is just so expensive these days. Maybe later.

Did you go to the "Know Your Religion" lecture? No, I wanted to, but three dollars a person is a little steep for my family. Besides, *Top Gun* cost us enough for that week. A year's supply of food? You must be kidding! I can't even afford the gas for my boat!

I've always wanted to go to Nauvoo and Independence and other church historical sites, and we are going to go as soon as we can afford it. ("All right, everybody, the water park opens in just two hours. Hurry, we'll be late!") Musical instruments for my kids? Too expensive! Anyway, we're still paying for their three-wheelers.

We can't afford to put in a garden this year, because seeds and fertilizer cost too much. But next year for sure! ("Honey, look here—the supermarket has tomatoes on special for 96 cents a pound!") You know, I'd like to fix up and beautify our home, but building expenses are out of sight. But we *did* buy a beautiful new TV, which looks very nice in our living room.

Boy, it's expensive being a good Latter-day Saint! There is always something to donate to. If things don't get better, I may have to sell my pool table to have enough to pay a fast offering. And talk about expensive—have you looked at the price of a colledge education? It's ridiculous! You know, I didn't pay much more than that as the down payment on our cabin at the lake. And missions—they say that one month of a typical mission now costs as much as our hunting lease and golf course membership combined! Yes, times *are* bad. There are many things we *can't* afford. But isn't it amazing how much we feel we can afford?

Let's not rationalize away the things we need to be doing with our families. Let's keep our priorities straight and set an example worthy to follow.

When times get really tough, I recall an experience I had while attending Ricks College. Because of a money shortage, my roommates and I got jobs in a potato cellar at harvest time. Our assignment was to use large pitchforks to shovel about thirty-five pounds of potatoes at a time onto a conveyor belt. Within thirty minutes we were breathing heavily, and within four hours one of my roommates had quit. After two more days, all the rest of my friends had quit. I continued for two reasons. One was the fact that I was broke. The other was that on the other side of the mounds of potatoes was a sixty-five-year-old man who had the same job that I had. Although he never said a word to me, his example got me through the experience. By the third day my arms were so sore that I could hardly lift them, but every time I wanted to quit, I would look up at that older man and say to myself, "There's no way I am going to let him get the best of me." And I would keep shoveling.

I soon learned a great lesson from that experience. I found that the more I shoveled the potatoes, the greater my capacity became to accomplish my task. Soon the soreness was gone, and I could shovel without tiring. In fact, I became so adept that I could beat the old man's production quite easily. The supervisors soon gave me a raise—although the pay remained the same. My new assignment was to carry 100-pound sacks from the conveyor belt to the storage rooms. So it was a raise in weight, instead of in pay. I quickly found out what real work was. I had just *thought* the shoveling was hard!

To our children, we should be like the old man in this story, always there working hard and setting a good example for them to follow. Often, children will go on to achieve even more than the parents who have set the example.

Sometimes as parents we get so keyed up about how hard it is to be a parent that we forget how hard it is to be a child. Children have tremendous amounts of pressure placed on them by society and even their own peers. Sometimes we are too quick to judge them by outer appearance or habits. They need example, encouragement, and teaching, not criticism.

Recently I stopped at a gas station to gas up my car. While the gas was pumping, a young man drove up, got out of his car, and started to pump gas also. He had a sloppy beard, was not dressed well, and hadn't combed his hair the way I thought he should, and I thought to myself with pride, *This poor boy just doesn't have it!* As I walked over to the cashier to pay my bill, I discovered I didn't have enough money with me. I explained my situation to the cashier, then went back to my car to search for some loose change, but soon found I had none. As I walked back to tell the cashier of my dilemma, the young man whom I had earlier judged walked past me and said, "Don't worry about it." I ignored his comment. But when I asked the cashier if she trusted me to go home and get the money, she said that the young man had seen what had happened and paid the bill for me. I ran back to the pump to get his address so I could pay him back, but he just said, "Don't worry about it," and drove off. I had never seen that boy before that day, nor have I seen him since, but he taught me a valuable lesson. Sometimes we are too quick to judge others. Sometimes we are even too quick to judge our own children. Let us remember that these are they who have been saved to come forth in this last dispensation to prepare the way for the Savior's second coming. Within our children are the seeds of greatness. Our responsibility is to help them recognize who they are so they can fulfill their divine destiny.

If we are to be successful in our callings as parents, we must pray for help and guidance. We are told, "Counsel with the Lord in all thy doings," and if we will do this, "he will direct [us] for good." (Alma 37:37.) I testify that prayer will help us guide our families safely through these trying times. But I believe that the Lord requires more than prayer. We pray that we will be great and noble parents and have successful families. The Lord then provides us with the opportunity of being parents. Whether we are successful or not depends on what we do with our opportunities. We have free agency. Are we putting forth the effort that it takes to learn how to have successful families? Or are we just praying that a miracle will happen?

Do we know where we are going as parents? Do we have family goals to achieve, or do we just go along and hope for the best? If we don't set family goals, how can we ever hope to achieve them? Achieving hard goals through prayer and work will bring much joy and happiness into our homes.

One of the hardest things my wife and I ever did was to help our second son, Nolan, reach a personal goal. He wanted to read the entire Book of Mormon before his eighth birthday. We realized what we had gotten into the very first day when we had to explain every single word in the first verse except the word *I*. It was a very slow and tedious process, and almost every day I wanted to quit. Day after day we read; hour after hour we explained the words he didn't know, and he would then repeat them. Then, after several months of reading, we all began to receive blessings. We found that Nolan was beginning to read more on his own. His reading skills were improving, and he was gaining a testimony of the Book of Mormon. Finally, the night before his birthday, he read the last verse of this great scripture, having completed his goal. I can't describe the feeling of joy that came into our home or the inspiration that came into our lives that night, but it was real. We had discovered that appropriate family goals will help us achieve what our Heavenly Father has sent us here to do. We also had reaffirmation of the power of the Book of Mormon to inspire us in achieving our mission.

President Ezra Taft Benson has given each of us a challenge to read the Book of Mormon daily, and has promised us great blessings if we will follow this counsel. In his first conference address as president of the Church, he quoted and endorsed the words of President Marion G. Romney:

If we would avoid adopting the evils of the world, we must pursue a course which will daily feed our minds with and call them back to the things of the spirit. I know of no better way to do this than by reading the Book of Mormon....

And so, I counsel you, my beloved brothers and sisters and friends everywhere, to make reading in the Book of Mormon a few minutes each day a lifelong practice.... I feel certain that if, in our homes, parents will read from the Book of Mormon prayerfully and regularly, both by themselves and with their children, the spirit of that great book will come to permeate our homes and all who dwell therein. The spirit of reverence will increase, mutual respect and consideration for each other will grow. The spirit of contention will depart. Parents will counsel their children in greater love and wisdom. Children will be more responsive and submissive to that counsel. Righteousness will increase. Faith, hope, and charity—the pure love of Christ—will abound in our homes and lives, bringing in their wake peace, joy, and happiness.[1]

The promises that were made concerning the blessings that will come to our families from our study of the Book of Mormon are almost too great to comprehend. I pray that we will all take this book seriously, use it as the guide for our families, follow its teachings, and then endure to the end. If we read it closely, it will lead us to a foundation that will not fall. Helaman gave us the key in his counsel to his sons: "And now my sons, remember, remember that it is upon the rock of our Redeemer, who is Christ, the Son of God, that ye must build your foundation, that when the devil shall send forth his mighty winds, yea, his shafts in the whirlwind, yea, when all his hail and his mighty storm shall beat upon you, it shall have no power over you to drag you down to the gulf of misery and endless wo, because of the rock upon which ye are built, which is a sure foundation, a foundation whereon if men build they cannot fall." (Helaman 5:12.)

NOTE

1. Marion G. Romney, "Drink Deeply from the Divine Fountain," *Improvement Era*, April 1960, p. 436.

INDEX

Accountability, 77-78, 112-13, 122-23
Activities, appropriate, requiring attendance at, 118
Advertisements, effectiveness of, 61
Age-guessing booth at fair, 15-16
Agency: helping children use, 117-18; parents are expected to exercise, 136
Alamo, memorial at, 36-37
Alcohol, use of, glamorized by television, 55-56
Alcoholic, poem written by, 20-21
Alvis, Letitia, 94
Apathy, danger of, 17
Army, author's induction into, 91
Athletic shoes, media advertising of, 32-33

Basics, importance of emphasizing, 127-28
Basketball player, lesson learned by, 120-21
Benson, Ezra Taft: on latter-day forces of evil, vii-viii; on improper media and entertainment, 11; on undesirable heroes, 36; on decline of media, 45; on recognizing and overcoming evil, 85; on reading Book of Mormon, 136-37
Blessings, priesthood, on birthdays, 124
Blue jeans, peer pressure illustrated by, 25-28
Book of Mormon: test about, 64; child sets goal to read, 136; Church members counseled to read, 136-37
Butler, Nicholas, 5

Candy company, success of, after movie tie-in, 78-79
Caughey, Dr. John, 28-29
Children, avoiding temptation to judge, 135
Church meetings, repetition of topics discussed in, 127-28
City council, debate in, over obscene material, 107-10
Cline, Dr. Victor L.: on media violence and aggressive behavior, 53; on effects of media on self-image, 80;

films analyzed by, 82-83; on pornography, 84
Communication, television as barrier to, 56-57
Community involvement against obscenity, 107-13
Complacency, danger of, 17
Concert, hard-rock: teenager's report on, 96-97; watching people arriving at, 99-100
"Continue Singing," musical game, 103
Cotton candy, story of, illustrating accountability, 112
Counsel: willingness to accept, 6-8; hearing, without applying, 115-16
Crime, possible influence of television on, 52-54

Dangers, spiritual, becoming oblivious to, 3-5
Dating, rules for, 125
Deception: practiced by junior high students, 13-14; people's unawareness of, 14-15; Satan's powers of, 14-15, 19, 21
Desensitization: TV's role in, 57; through repeated exposure, 74; to profanity, 74-76
Dew, Sheri L., 11
Discipline problems in schools, 9-10

Example, importance of setting, 134
Exposure: role of, in developing likes and dislikes, 36, 65; creates desensitization, 74

False Christs and prophets, 17-18
Families: increased pressures on, vii-viii; protecting, against improper movies, 85; establishing guidelines in, for movie viewing, 86-89; writing original song for, 102; interviews in, 123; having goals for, 136
Father's blessings, 124
Financial priorities, 132-34
Foundations, spiritual, learning to check, viii

Games promoting good music, 103
Gas station, stranger pays bill at, 135
Goals: setting, 121-22; being accountable for, 122-23; for parents, 136
Go-cart accident, 1-2
Grapes, sampling, at supermarket, 129-30

Heroes: listed in national polls, 28-30; generally undesirable traits of, 30, 36; real, exposing families to, 35-36
Hinckley, Gordon B., on lifestyles of TV personalities, 43-44
Holy Ghost, following guidance of, 8
Hymnbook, carrying, in car, 102
Hymns, learning background of, 103

INDEX 141

Imitating TV characters, 60-61
Immorality: influence of television on, 54-55; increase of, in movies, 81; as topic of music, 95-96; goals as barrier to, 121-22
Impatience generated by television viewing, 59-60
Interviews with family members, 123
Irreverence, family home evening lesson on, 130-32

Jewels, child likened to, 3
Judgment: by intents of heart, 77-78; none will escape, 112-13; avoiding temptations to pronounce, 135
Jump, Gordon, 10

Kimball, Spencer W.: on spiritual lethargy, 4-5; on following prophets, 8; on inviting nature of sin, 18; on recurrence of days of Satan, 49; on shunning pornography, 83-84; on fighting pornography, 105, 106; on sex education in home, 123; on steady dating, 125
Kindergarten, bribing child to attend, 116-17
Kiss, bedtime, 123

Latter-day Saints: are subject to deception, 15; heroes of youth of, match national polls, 29
Latter days, increased leisure time in, vii

Lee, Harold B., on following the Brethren, 5-6
Lehi's vision of tree of life, 34-35
Levi's, peer pressure illustrated by, 25-28
Lie-detector test, youth's experience with, 119

Marble game, boys deceive teachers with, 13-14
Media: power of, 10; deterioration of standards in, 10; Satan's ability to use, 10-11; imaginary relationships developed with, 28-29; heroes created by, 29; profanity promulgated by, 31-32; power of, in promoting certain products, 32-33, 61; decline of, 45; controlling, to promote moral cleanliness, 126
Merrill, Kieth, 10
Mocking, 33-35
Moral cleanliness: requires goals and encouragement, 117; role of self-esteem in, 119-21; role of goal setting in, 121-23; dating rules designed to promote, 125
Moroni, counsel of, on recognizing good and evil, 88
Motion Picture Association of America, 82
Movies: selecting, on friends' recommendations, 73-74; profanity and immorality in,

74-76; inappropriate, rationalizations for seeing, 76-77; content of, is ultimately determined by audience, 78; candy company tie-in with, 78-79; likened to improper party, 80; rating of, by Motion Picture Association, 81-82; major audience for, is under age thirty, 85; guidelines for selecting, 87-89; rating, as a family board, 88; obscene, accessibility of, to minors, 108

Murrow, Edward R., 63

Music: power of, illustrated by army example, 91-92; power of, shown throughout history, 92; repetition of, is enjoyable, 93; in enhancing memory, 93-95; Satan's deadly use of, 95; immoral messages in, 95-96; can drive out or invite Spirit, 97-98; describing typical audiences for different types of, 98-99; creating different moods with, 99; inappropriate, weaning family away from, 100-101; good, exposure to, 100; good, increasing appreciation for, 100-104; building library of, 101-2, analyzing different types of, 102-3

"Musical Hash," musical game, 103

Musical instruments, learning to play, 102, 120

"Name That Tune," musical game, 103

Nutrition, TV's effect on, 57-58

Obscenity: walking out on, 87; responsibility to fight, 105-7, 112; battle over, in city council, 107-10; ideas for combatting, in community, 110-11

Packard, David, 94

Parents: training role of, 2-3; roles of, as modeled on TV, 61; requiring permission of, for movie viewing, 87; responsibilities of, to dictate some decisions, 118-19; should wait up for children, 123-24; difficult task of, 129; must set example, 134; must pray for help and guidance, 135-36

Peer pressure: at water slide, 23-24; Satan's use of, 25; illustrated by styles of blue jeans, 25-28; in form of mocking, 33-35; self-esteem helps children withstand, 35

Plain-pocket jeans, peer pressure illustrated by, 25-28

Pope, Alexander, 76

Pornography: true definition of, 83; difficult to erase from mind, 83-84; effects of viewing, 84

Prayer, parents must rely on, 135-36

Present that was gift-wrapped with money, 18-19

Primary class lesson on influence of television, 51-52
Problems, seeking solutions to, 129, 132
Profanity: counting instances of, 30-32; becoming desensitized to, 74-76
Prophets: safety in following, 5-6; resolving to follow counsel of, 11-12

Rape prevention conference, 115-16
Ratings for movies, 82-83
Rationalization, 76-77
Romney, Marion G., 136-37
Rules for TV viewing, 67-68

Satan: latter-day tools of, vii-viii, 5; power of, to deceive, 14-15, 19, 21; uses peer pressure to entice to sin, 25; power of, repeated through history, 49; music as deadly tool of, 95
School: discipline problems in, comparison of, 9; most effective type of, 39; performance in, affects of television on, 56
Self-esteem: effects of, on peer pressure, 35; role of, in staying morally clean, 119-21
Sin: diverse forms of, ix; is made to look inviting, 17-18; small, can become significant, 129-30
Smith, Joseph, 92, 104
Smith, Joseph Fielding, 85
Smokeless tobacco, 32

Spa, analogy of, 86
Streaker, story of, illustrating accountability, 77

Taylor, John, 15
Teaching moments, being alert to, 130
Teenagers: importance of training of, 2-3; heroes of, 28-30; pacesetters among, 33; rise in pregnancies among, 54; waiting up for, 123-24
Television: likened to school system, 39-44; community involvement in, 40-41; life-styles of stars of, 43-44; decline in quality of, 45-46; positive potential of, 45, 63; monitoring, 46-48; negative behaviors on, 47; positive behaviors on, 48; Primary children illustrate influence of, 51-52; violence on, 52-54; immorality on, 54-55; alcohol glamorized on, 55-56; effects of, on academic performance, 56; as barrier to communication, 56-57; desensitizes, 57; promotes unhealthful foods, 57-58; consumes time, 58-59; effects of, on attention span, 59; creates impatience with real-life situations, 59-60; and career expectations, 60; poor role models on, 60-61; erodes age distinctions, 61-62; addictive properties of, 62; distracts from important issues, 62; and

physical fitness, 62; fears produced by, 62; medium of, is neutral, 63; wise use of, 63; test to family's watching habits, 64; questionnaire on family use of, 65; unplugging, 66; family rules governing, 66-68; positive aspects of, 68-69; controlling time spent with, 69-70

Temptations: instructing children in dealing with, 2-3; becoming aware of, 5; likened to traffic on busy street, 6-8; in media, 11; inviting nature of, is deceptive, 17; as "false prophets," 18

Tiffany's, man's experience in, 3

Tornado warning, 8-9

Travis, Colonel William, 36-37

Tree of life, Lehi's vision of, 34-35

Trust does not alleviate need for protection, 117, 125-26

Videocassette recorders, 79-80

Violence: influence of television on, 52-54; desensitization to, 57; in movies, 81

Water slide, peer pressure at, 23-24

Whetmore, Edward Jay, 95

Wold, Eric, 119

Woodruff, Wilford, 11

Work, setting example in, 134